HOUSE OF

European Union Committee

23rd Report of Session 2007–08

The Commission's Annual Policy Strategy for 2009

Report with Evidence

Ordered to be printed 15 July 2008 and published 23 July 2008

Published by the Authority of the House of Lords

London : The Stationery Office Limited
£13.50

HL Paper 151

The European Union Committee

The European Union Committee is appointed by the House of Lords "to consider European Union documents and other matters relating to the European Union". The Committee has seven Sub-Committees which are:
Economic and Financial Affairs, and International Trade (Sub-Committee A)
Internal Market (Sub-Committee B)
Foreign Affairs, Defence and Development Policy (Sub-Committee C)
Environment and Agriculture (Sub-Committee D)
Law and Institutions (Sub-Committee E)
Home Affairs (Sub-Committee F)
Social and Consumer Affairs (Sub-Committee G)

Our Membership

The Members of the European Union Committee are:

Lord Blackwell
Baroness Cohen of Pimlico
Lord Dykes
Lord Freeman
Lord Grenfell (Chairman)
Lord Harrison
Baroness Howarth of Breckland
Lord Jopling
Lord Kerr of Kinlochard
Lord Maclennan of Rogart

Lord Mance
Lord Plumb
Lord Powell of Bayswater
Lord Roper
Lord Sewel
Baroness Symons of Vernham Dean
Lord Tomlinson
Lord Wade of Chorlton
Lord Wright of Richmond

Information about the Committee

The reports and evidence of the Committee are published by and available from The Stationery Office. For information freely available on the web, our homepage is:
http://www.parliament.uk/parliamentary_committees/lords_eu_select_committee.cfm
There you will find many of our publications, along with press notices, details of membership and forthcoming meetings, and other information about the ongoing work of the Committee and its Sub-Committees, each of which has its own homepage.
Members' interests are available at the Register of Interests:
http://www.parliament.uk/about_lords/register_of_lords__interests.cfm

Contacts for the European Union Committee

Contact details for individual Sub-Committees are given on the website.
General correspondence should be addressed to the Clerk of the European Union Committee, Committee Office, House of Lords, London, SW1A 0PW
The telephone number for general enquiries is 020 7219 5791.The Committee's email address is euclords@parliament.uk

CONTENTS

NOTE: References in the text of the report are as follows:
(Q) refers to a question in oral evidence
(p) refers to a page in written evidence

FOREWORD—what this Report is about

In this report, we set out our views on the Annual Policy Strategy for 2009, in which the Commission describes its priorities and plans for the coming year. The Annual Policy Strategy gives us the opportunity to scrutinise the Commission's intentions as early in the legislative process as possible.

Given the fact that a new college of Commissioners will be appointed in November 2009, we comment on the Commission's overarching priorities for next year. We give our preliminary views on some of the Commission's plans, considering whether the Commission's proposed action is appropriate and achievable. We aim to influence the Commission's Legislative and Work Programme, which will be published in the autumn and will set out detailed plans for 2009 on the basis of dialogue on the Annual Policy Strategy.

We examine what the Commission says in the Annual Policy Strategy about its better regulation agenda and communication priorities for 2009. We also scrutinise the Commission's proposed allocation of personnel and funding, and comment on whether the Commission seems to be backing up its priorities with real resources.

We discuss the Annual Policy Strategy as a consultation document, including whether there is enough clarity about the document's purpose. Finally, we express our views on whether the Government gives sufficient attention to the Annual Policy Strategy.

The Commission's Annual Policy Strategy for 2009

CHAPTER 1: INTRODUCTION

What is the Commission's Annual Policy Strategy?

1. The Annual Policy Strategy is one of the two key strategic planning documents published by the European Commission each year. The Annual Policy Strategy (or APS) published in the spring sets out the Commission's priorities for the following year, and forms the basis for discussion within the EU institutions and beyond. This discussion is intended to influence the Commission's Annual Legislative and Work Programme, published in the autumn, which fleshes out those priorities and sets out detailed plans for the year ahead.

Our report

2. This report sets out our views on the Annual Policy Strategy for 2009.[1] The Annual Policy Strategy gives us the opportunity to scrutinise the Commission's intentions as early in the legislative process as possible. Given the fact that a new college of Commissioners will be appointed in November 2009, we comment on the Commission's overarching priorities for the coming year. We express our preliminary views on some of the Commission's plans, looking at whether the Commission's proposed action is appropriate and achievable, with the aim of influencing the Commission's Annual Legislative and Work Programme for 2009. We also examine the Commission's better regulation agenda and communication priorities, and scrutinise the Commission's proposed allocation of financial and human resources. Finally, we discuss the Annual Policy Strategy as a consultation document, including whether there is enough clarity about the document's purpose, and whether the Government gives it sufficient attention.

3. We thank Jim Murphy MP, Minister for Europe, and Commissioner Margot Wallström, Commission Vice-President and Commissioner for Institutional Relations and Communication Strategy, for providing us with both written and oral evidence. We make this report to the House for debate.

---

[1] The Commission's Annual Policy Strategy for 2009 (Communication from the Commission to the European Parliament, the Council, the European Economic and Social Committee and the Committee of the Regions: Annual Policy Strategy for 2009 (COM(2008) 72 final)) is available at http://ec.europa.eu/atwork/synthesis/index_en.htm.

CHAPTER 2: A YEAR OF CHANGES AT THE TOP

4. The Commission's Annual Policy Strategy for 2009, published on 18 February 2008, looks ahead to a year which will see a new European Parliament elected in June and a new college of Commissioners appointed in November.[2] The election means that the majority of legislative business should ideally be concluded by May 2009. The Commission will have tabled most of its major outstanding legislative initiatives by the end of 2008, meaning that a considerable lull in the presentation of legislative proposals is foreseen for next year. During 2009, the Commission indicates that it will focus on reaching agreement on these initiatives, on implementation of the *acquis*, and on effective financial management.[3]

5. At the time of publication, the Commission also looked forward to the Lisbon Treaty's entry into force at the beginning of 2009, if it had been ratified by all 27 Member States. Preparations were being made to ensure the smooth implementation of the Treaty's changes to the European institutions when it was announced that Ireland had voted "no" to the Treaty in its referendum of 12 June 2008. The picture has therefore changed since the Annual Policy Strategy was published and since the Commission wrote that "[w]ith a stable institutional framework in place, the Union will be able to concentrate on addressing the concrete challenges ahead".[4]

6. The Commission Vice-President in charge of institutional relations and communication, Margot Wallström, said that the referendum result would have "no direct consequences" on the schedule for both the European Parliament elections and the Commission change-over in 2009. The Annual Policy Strategy "took a prudent approach" to the Lisbon Treaty and did not list all the consequences of its entry into force or the initiatives flowing from it. The Commissioner said that "[t]he nature and timing of such initiatives will clearly be subject to ongoing review" (p 14). She indicated that a number of implementation measures were on hold, and said that at present "everybody prefers not to engage in some kind of alternative plan but focus on ratification and solving the problems that we see right now" (Q 43). She did not say that the priorities in the Annual Policy Strategy would be substantially affected, although the details of policy proposals in areas that would have been significantly altered by the Lisbon Treaty's implementation, such as the area of freedom, security and justice, may well change. Much may depend on what the Taoiseach tells the European Council in October about the Lisbon Treaty's future.

7. Because of the disruption caused by the arrival of a new European Parliament and a new Commission in 2009, the majority of the initiatives included in the Annual Policy Strategy are either non-legislative or implement legislation that has already been adopted. The "key actions" for 2009 listed in the Annual Policy Strategy's annex include stocktakings, communications, green papers, follow-ups, progress reports and action plans.[5] **We welcome the Commission's agenda of consolidation for 2009 as pragmatic.**

---

[2] Annual Policy Strategy p 3

[3] Annual Policy Strategy p 3

[4] Annual Policy Strategy p 3

[5] Annual Policy Strategy Annex, pp 14–18

8.   **We think that the legislative lull in 2009 provides an excellent opportunity for the Commission to focus on the even-handed implementation of EU legislation across the Member States. That some of the 850 Commission posts to be newly created or redeployed in 2009 will be allocated to supporting the implementation of the *acquis* also reflects a welcome degree of commitment to this agenda.**

CHAPTER 3: THE COMMISSION'S PRIORITIES

9. In this final year of the Barroso Commission, the four strategic objectives defined in 2005 at the start of the Commission's five-year term—promoting prosperity, solidarity, security and freedom, and Europe as a world partner—remain the "core direction" for the Commission's work.[6] The Annual Policy Strategy specifies five priority areas for the Commission in 2009: "Growth and Jobs", "Climate Change and Sustainable Europe", "Making a Reality of the Common Immigration Policy", "Putting the Citizen First", and "Europe as a World Partner".[7]

10. Commissioner Wallström told us that in 2009 "the Commission will stick to its ambition of delivering a Europe of results and bringing concrete benefits to citizens" (Q 34). She explained, "[w]e win democratic legitimacy by doing the right things that really change the lives of European citizens" (Q 61). The Government said in its Explanatory Memorandum on the Annual Policy Strategy that it agreed with the Commission that "it is important that the EU focuses on delivering recognisable benefits and tangible policies that matter to its citizens"[8] (see also p 13). **We agree with the Commission's objective of delivering results on issues that concern citizens, and to communicate those results. The Commission's priorities should be based on the question of what makes the European Union relevant to the people of Europe.**

11. The Commission told us that including "Putting the Citizen First"[9] as a priority "reflects the fact that one of the main objectives of this Commission is to put the citizen at the centre of the European project and to deliver policies which are relevant to their everyday lives" (p 14). The proposals put forward under the heading "Putting the Citizen First" cover the free movement of European citizens, the common area of justice, security and civil protection, public health, food safety, animal health and welfare, consumer product safety rules, chemicals regulation, flexicurity, youth, health and safety at work, gender equality, anti-discrimination and inclusion. **We welcome the priority on "Putting the Citizen First", but regret the lack of coherence among the disparate sub-priorities gathered underneath this heading. The Commission should do more to stress the weight it places on putting the citizen first throughout its work, thereby giving more coherence to this list of sub-priorities. Particular attention should be paid to issues impacting on communities and local projects.**

12. Asked about the Government's priorities within those outlined by the Commission, the Minister for Europe, Jim Murphy MP, highlighted "climate change, not least for the geopolitical reasons ... if Europe either reneges on its commitment on renewables and other aspects of the climate change package or gives the impression of being luke warm I think it will send

---

[6] Annual Policy Strategy p 3

[7] Annual Policy Strategy pp 4–7

[8] The Government's Explanatory Memoranda on European Union documents are available at http://europeanmemorandum.cabinetoffice.gov.uk/search.aspx.
The Government's Explanatory Memorandum on the Annual Policy Strategy for 2009 is available at http://europeanmemorandum.cabinetoffice.gov.uk/memo_details.aspx?mcmoID=1207.

[9] Annual Policy Strategy pp 5–6

a signal to other groups of nations across the planet and would have a negative impact on other world capitals, not least in Brazil, Russia, Washington and elsewhere" (Q 3). **We welcome the Commission's focus on climate change, as crucial both to Europe's future and to connecting the EU with its citizens.[10] Once the EU has agreed its package of energy and climate change measures[11], which it has agreed to do by early 2009 at the latest, the EU must strive for an environmentally and economically sustainable deal at the United Nations Climate Change Conference in Copenhagen in December 2009.**

13. **The emphasis on "Europe as a World Partner" is also welcome, as the European Union must be in a position to address the challenges of a changing world in which China, India, Russia and other major powers and regions are rapidly playing a more important role.[12]**

14. **Delivering growth and jobs will also be fundamental to the role of the European Union in 2009, so we are glad to see it prioritised.[13]**

15. Regarding immigration, the Commissioner, in her written evidence, cited the European Council's December 2007 conclusion that "further developing this policy—which complements Member States' policies—remains a fundamental priority in order to meet the challenges and harness the opportunities which migration represents in a new era of globalisation". She added: "A Common Immigration Policy is the best and in many cases the only way to address a number of very significant problems such as shrinking EU population and demographic ageing, labour and skills shortages, insufficient integration of legal immigrants, continuous pressure of illegal immigration, insufficient partnership with third countries or insufficient adaptation of border management and visa policy to the needs of a globalized world" (p 13). **The Commission's prioritisation of immigration reflects the importance most Member States attach to this issue and the priorities set by the Council.[14] We welcome the collective efforts to tackle what is currently one of the major challenges facing the EU as a whole. We note, however, that the issue of immigration is far from uncontroversial for some Member States (particularly the United Kingdom, which has the right to choose whether to participate (the opt-in) in this area) and the Commission will need to handle this priority carefully, giving due regard to the principles of subsidiarity and proportionality and thereby showing that specific measures in this field add value.**

16. We think that the Commission's efforts on trade should be more visible in the Commission's Annual Policy Strategy, given the importance that the Commission attaches to the World Trade Organisation negotiations and the

---

[10] Annual Policy Strategy p 5

[11] Communication from the Commission "20 20 by 2020—Europe's climate change opportunity" (COM(2008) 30, 23 January 2008. In addition to the non-legislative Communication, the package of measures published on the same day included legislative proposals on the emissions trade scheme (COM(2008) 16), emissions reductions outside the emissions trading scheme (COM(2008) 17), carbon capture and storage (COM(2008) 18) and renewable energy (COM(2008) 19).

[12] Annual Policy Strategy pp 6–7

[13] Annual Policy Strategy p 4

[14] Annual Policy Strategy p 5

increasing strength of emerging economies such as China and India. **Given the critical importance of trade, the hazardous condition of World Trade Organisation negotiations and the rising protectionist threat in various parts of the world, the Commission should make sure that trade is a priority for 2009.**

CHAPTER 4: THE DETAILS OF THE ANNUAL POLICY STRATEGY PRIORITIES

"Growth and Jobs"

17. The Commission says that "[p]romoting sustainable economic and social reform in Europe under the renewed Lisbon Strategy for growth and jobs will continue to be at the heart of the Commission's political agenda."[15] The Lisbon Strategy, agreed in 2000 and refreshed in 2005, aims to make the European Union the most competitive economy in the world and to achieve full employment by 2010. Competitiveness will be crucial to the EU's prosperity, so **we encourage the Commission to keep up the momentum on the Lisbon Strategy.**[16]

18. The Commission's Annual Policy Strategy makes three references to the current global financial situation, saying: "The impact of the global financial turbulence on the real economy and the hike in raw material prices will require the EU to deepen its structural reforms at both EU and national level"; "The Commission will actively engage in the response to the global financial turbulence, which will require long-term adjustments in the regulatory and supervisory environment for financial services"; and "The current financial turmoil calls for a coordinated EU response, including a stronger presence of the Commission in international financial institutions."[17]

19. The Commissioner told us that the Finance Ministers of the G7 and Commissioner Almunia (Commissioner for Economic and Monetary Affairs) had reaffirmed their support for the International Monetary Fund to work closely with other international bodies, especially the Financial Stability Forum.[18] They expressed their support for the Commission becoming an observer of the Financial Stability Forum, because of the overlap between the Forum's work and the work programme endorsed by the ECOFIN Council, and so that it could act as a co-ordinator between the G7 and the EU in this area (pp 14-15). The Commission's position was that it wanted observer status, and was "looking for support from the Member States for that" (Q 48). The Commissioner pointed out that the Commission has observer status in the Basel Committee on Banking Supervision (p 15), and also that the Commission could not act beyond the competences granted to it in the Treaties, including in its work in international financial institutions (Q 53).

20. The Minister for Europe commented that "[i]n terms of the role of Europe in these international debates and international institutions ... there is a role for the Commission, although the exact shape and nature of that role is open to conjecture and continued discussion" (Q 18). **There will need to be**

---

[15] Annual Policy Strategy p 4

[16] See European Union Committee, 28th Report (2005–06): *A European Strategy for Jobs and Growth* (HL 137).

[17] Annual Policy Strategy pp 4, 6

[18] The Financial Stability Forum was convened in April 1999 to promote international financial stability through information exchange and international co-operation in financial supervision and surveillance. Membership includes senior representatives of national financial authorities (e.g. central banks, supervisory authorities and treasury departments), international financial institutions, international regulatory and supervisory groupings, committees of central bank experts and the European Central Bank.

careful consideration and case-by-case justification of any enhanced Commission role in international financial institutions.

21.   The Annual Policy Strategy states that the Commission will assist the European Institute for Innovation and Technology (EIT) in its first year of full operation.[19] The EIT was set up by Regulation (EC) No 294/2008 of the European Parliament and of the Council of 11 March 2008. Its aim is to encourage and facilitate networking and cooperation between universities, research and business communities working in fields that are considered to represent "strategic long-term challenges for innovation in Europe", such as climate change.[20] **We look forward to seeing detail in the Annual Legislative and Work Programme about the ways in which the Commission will assist the EIT.** Given the importance placed by the Commission on "Putting the Citizen First", **we stress to the Government and the Commission the importance of ensuring the involvement of the private sector, most notably at the local level.**[21] It is important that the EIT maintains and develops local projects and thereby helps Europe become more understood by local communities.

22.   The Minister told us: "[t]he purpose of the European Institute, in my understanding, is to be a European hub of innovation, it is not to create a research and development monster and it is not to suck up capacity and expertise that already exists in other European capitals, and … in different regions and towns and cities throughout the European Union" (Q 9). **We urge the Government to seek to ensure that this purpose is followed in the development of the EIT.**

23.   We note that the Annual Policy Strategy forecasts a 2009 Communication on sectoral social dialogue and its contribution to the Lisbon Strategy.[22] Sectoral social dialogue is dialogue between employers and employees on a sector-by-sector basis. **We are grateful for the Commission's clarification of the background to this proposal and welcome it on that basis (p 18).**

"Climate Change and Sustainable Europe"

24.   2009 will be an important year for climate change work, including the finalisation of the 2008 climate change and energy package with a view to formulating a robust EU position at the Copenhagen climate change talks (December 2009).[23] The Minister told us that the conversation on climate change and energy was "pretty lively" in some capitals. The issue of "carbon leakage" was important. This refers to the transfer of investment opportunities to countries "with a less rigorous climate change regime", with the effect of increasing emissions in the destination countries. He concluded, "Her Majesty's Government is very strongly of the view that the solution to

---

[19] Annual Policy Strategy p 4; see European Union Committee, 25th Report (2006–07): *Proposal to establish the European Institute of Technology* (HL 130).

[20] Recital 7 of the adopted Regulation (294/2008)

[21] The private sector is important in the context of the EIT because one of its stated priorities is to transfer knowledge to the business context, as well as to support the creation of start-ups, spin-offs and small and medium-sized enterprises (SMEs). In our Report on the proposal (European Union Committee, 25th Report (2006–07): *Proposal to establish the European Institute of Technology* (HL 130)), we took the view that "the only way to assess effectively whether or not the EIT is successfully achieving the objectives for which it is intended will be to look closely at the business impact of its activities at local level".

[22] Annual Policy Strategy p 14

[23] Annual Policy Strategy p 5

this is not a carbon tariff or a protectionist tariff of any sort, because it is pretty dangerous if the international message is that the only way you can do the right thing on climate change is by virtue of a new round of tariffs, and it would lead very quickly to retaliatory measures" (Q 17). **We agree that the EU must not attempt to tackle the climate change challenge by applying protectionist measures.**

25.   We asked the Commissioner about EU action on high prices for fuel and for food. She told us that "[t]hese matters are at the top of the political agenda in all the Member States right now … it is extremely important" (Q 51). She indicated that discussions at the June European Council had shown "the importance of finding the right balance" between "responding quickly to a genuine problem", and "acknowledging the deeper challenge of adjusting to new realities for the long term". She added that Commission action in the area of energy prices would include a package of measures to help fishermen face the need to restructure, and proposals on emergency and commercial oil stocks. The Commission and the French Presidency (which runs from 1 July 2008 to 31 December 2008) will report on the feasibility and impact of "measures to smooth the effects of the sudden price increases" to the October 2008 European Council, and the Commission will report to the European Council on food and oil price developments in Europe and internationally in December 2008 (p 16). **We note the Commission's efforts in this area, and urge the Commission, in their forthcoming work, to take into account changing views regarding the use of biofuels.**

26.   The Commissioner made the connection between high energy prices, energy security and climate change. Agreeing the proposed EU policy on climate change and renewables would lead to reduced oil and gas consumption, and therefore increased energy security. She said that it was important to promote competition in energy markets, enhance dialogue with oil exporting countries, and improve the conditions for investment in oil exploration, production and refining. The Commission is working on the external aspects of energy security for a discussion at the December European Council (p 16). We note that energy security is also a priority of the French Presidency (see QQ 36, 51). **This is exactly the sort of issue that the Commission needs to prioritise: where Member States are stronger together, and where it really matters to citizens. We encourage the Commission's efforts in this area and note the legislative initiatives it has undertaken to tackle climate change, and to reduce CO_2 emissions and dependence on oil by promoting the use of renewable sources of energy.**[24]

27.   We will take a close interest in the Commission's work on climate change in 2008 and 2009. Our Internal Market Sub-Committee, Sub-Committee B, is conducting an inquiry into the EU's renewable energy target. Our Environment and Agriculture Sub-Committee, Sub-Committee D, is undertaking a short inquiry into the Commission's proposal for a revised EU Emissions Trading Scheme. Sub-Committee B will follow carefully the proposals to reduce greenhouse gas emissions from freight transport, including emissions from ships, included in the Annual Policy Strategy. It

---

[24] Sub-Committee B is conducting an inquiry into the EU's 20% renewable energy target; a report will be published in the autumn of 2008.

will also monitor the development of the Energy Policy for Europe which will lead to a new Energy Action Plan for the years 2010-2014.[25]

28. The Commission expects, in 2009, to implement the results of agreement planned for late 2008 on the "Health Check" of the Common Agricultural Policy (CAP).[26] The CAP "Health Check" is a mid-term review of the Common Agricultural Policy. On the basis of experience since the 2003 reform of the CAP, the Commission has proposed a number of changes that are intended to improve the 2003 reform Regulation without proposing more fundamental reform. The Minister, commenting on the CAP, told us: "the health check is important in terms of looking to simplify the single payment scheme and other farming and agricultural reforms, and it is also important, secondly, to have a conversation about the longer term. But we are very firm that the health check should not be used to set a longer term strategy on agricultural reform which is limited in its ambition. It has to be a wholesale reform of the Common Agricultural Policy ... There can be in a health check specific improvements but it is not a replacement for a wider reform of the Common Agricultural Policy ... I know there is a temptation in some European capitals for that to happen" (Q 17). **We support the Government in this long-term ambition for fundamental CAP reform, and we urge the Commission to ensure that the Health Check agreement is implemented promptly and effectively in the course of 2009.**

29. The Commission says in the Annual Policy Strategy that "[w]ork on the quality of agricultural products will continue", and Sub-Committee D is likely to take a strong interest in the Green Paper and Communication on Agricultural Product Quality that the Commission forecasts.[27] **We consider that the Commission's work on agricultural product quality must assist, rather than impede, progress towards improving the market orientation of the Common Agricultural Policy.**

30. The Commission includes in its list of key actions an action plan to develop a European Marine Observation and Data Network.[28] The Network will seek to be a "source of primary and processed data that can serve both public institutions, including their researchers, and commercial providers".[29] **A European Marine Observation and Data Network could be crucial in delivering an integrated marine policy and the Commission should concentrate on its careful design in order to ensure efficacy and avoid duplication of Member States' efforts.**

31. The Annual Policy Strategy says that in 2009 the Commission will submit a proposal on the reform of the Common Market Organisation (CMO) for fisheries and aquaculture products.[30] The CMO regulates aspects of the market by applying marketing standards, rules on consumer information, rules on Producer Organisations, and provisions relating to prices,

---

[25] Annual Policy Strategy pp 5, 15

[26] COM(2008) 306, 20 May 2008. The package of documents and further information can be found at http://ec.europa.eu/agriculture/healthcheck/index_en.htm.

[27] Annual Policy Strategy p 5

[28] Annual Policy Strategy p 16

[29] European Marine Observation and Data Network (EMODN) Background Paper No. 4a of the Maritime Green Paper Consultation Process. SEC(2006) 689, p 2.

[30] Annual Policy Strategy p 5

intervention and tariffs. The Commission explained that the CMO is currently undergoing a comprehensive evaluation which may result in proposals for its reform (p 17). The Government "firmly supports further reform, which is long overdue" (p 12).

32.   We have considered whether the fisheries and aquaculture CMO reform initiative might provide an opportunity to make further progress on eco-labelling of fisheries products. The Government agreed that "[r]eform will also be an opportunity for a greater focus on the consumption end of the fisheries marketing chain, linked to the promotion of fish as a healthy food source ... eco-labelling will be a key element of this". The Government "fully supports the principle of improving consumer information to assist purchasing decisions" (p 12). The Commissioner told us that the Commission plans to put forward a proposal for a new "Public/Private Partnership" in early 2009, "to stimulate the creation of a sector-driven European standard for both wild fisheries products and aquaculture", which would "produce the minimum EU requirements for Eco-labels" and "provide the minimum principles for certification and accreditation which would remain Member State competence". EU legislation may or may not be needed, and stakeholders will be invited to participate. "The aim is to have a scheme based on a real partnership with industry and civil society which will be responsive and easily adaptable to the needs of the industry (from fishermen to retailers) but take account of civil society aspirations" (p 17). **We support and encourage Commission initiatives to ensure that fisheries policy reflects the potential contribution that consumers can make in determining the sustainability or otherwise of EU fisheries, predominantly through clear, accurate and intelligible information provision.**

"Making a Reality of the Common Immigration Policy"

33.   Home affairs, particularly border management and immigration, continue to be high priorities for the Commission, and are one of France's top priorities for its Presidency.[31] The Government, in its Explanatory Memorandum, concurs with the Commission that "implementing the Global Approach to Migration remains a priority".[32] The EU's Global Approach to Migration was agreed by the European Council in December 2005, and brings together migration, external relations and development policy to address migration in an integrated, comprehensive and balanced way in partnership with third countries. The Commissioner told us that the idea of an immigration pact would be "part of the agenda where we now have to co-ordinate with the French Presidency" (Q 47). Some of the initiatives promoted by the Commission, such as EUROSUR and the entry/exit system, have significant legal, social, financial and human rights implications.[33] **These implications need to be analysed and published for consultation before any legislative proposal is brought forward, along with the Commission's other impact assessment work focussing on the technical feasibility of these initiatives. Consideration is also needed as to whether any**

---

[31]   Annual Policy Strategy p 5

[32]   See the Government's Explanatory Memorandum on the Annual Policy Strategy for 2009 at http://europeanmemorandum.cabinetoffice.gov.uk/memo_details.aspx?memoID=1207.

[33]   Annual Policy Strategy p 5

legislative proposals will meet the subsidiarity test and respect the proportionality principle.

"Putting the Citizen First"

34. The Commission says that in 2009, specific attention will be given to combating the risk of terrorist attacks in areas such as chemical, biological, nuclear and radiological threats.[34] **We endorse the shift of focus to specific threats,** which is entirely reasonable after much effort was concentrated on achieving further convergence on criminal law aspects which assist the fight against terrorism.[35]

35. While some measures, such as the work on consular protection, may enhance citizens' rights, there is no strong focus on fundamental rights in the Annual Policy Strategy.[36] While the protection of fundamental rights, as an aim in itself, is not the focus of the work of the EU (particularly given the role of the Council of Europe in this area) **fundamental rights should have a more evident role in shaping policy. We would expect the Annual Policy Strategy, in discussing policies in areas affecting security and fundamental rights—such as immigration and criminal justice—to flag up human rights concerns and engage in a preliminary discussion of issues raised.**

36. When asked which of the Commission's priorities the Government considered most important, the Minister told us that one of the top three would be "a watching brief on justice and home affairs" (Q 3). When asked whether the "area of freedom, security and justice" was a priority for the Commission, the Minister replied that the contents of the Annual Policy Strategy were "a reflection of a degree of vigilance by Her Majesty's Government which is continually arguing the case for mutual recognition rather than harmonisation". He agreed that "[o]n the issue of fundamental freedoms and justice and home affairs … the Annual Policy Strategy is relatively light", and he said that this was "largely because much of the work is contained in the five-year Hague Programme[37] of work, so most of the justice and home affairs issues are on-going as part of the four previous annual policy strategies" (Q 25). Civil and criminal justice do not receive much attention in the Annual Policy Strategy.[38] The Commission seems to envisage implementing what it can of the existing Hague Programme in 2009. The discussion of the successor of the Hague Programme is likely to provide a focus for a greater engagement with priority-setting in this area.

37. In written evidence, the Commission gave us more detail on its plans in the areas of civil and criminal justice (see pp 17–18): given the problems encountered in the implementation of the criminal justice aspects of the Hague Programme[39], we would have welcomed more detail in the Annual

---

[34] Annual Policy Strategy p 6

[35] For example, a package of measures adopted by the Commission in November 2007 included amendments to the Framework Decision on combating terrorism (14960/07).

[36] Annual Policy Strategy p 17

[37] The Hague Programme is a multiannual framework programme in the area of justice and home affairs for 2005–09.

[38] Annual Policy Strategy pp 5–6, 17

[39] For example, the failure of the Member States to reach agreement on the proposal for a Framework Decision on procedural rights in criminal proceedings and the absence of Commission proposals to date in the areas of admissibility of evidence and conflicts of jurisdiction and *ne bis in idem.*

Policy Strategy as to which aspects of the Hague Programme would be focussed upon. **While multiannual frameworks are important in the area of justice and home affairs, we would in future expect to see discussion in the Annual Policy Strategy, drawing on the multiannual framework, of the intended focus of the Commission's efforts in this field during the following year. We look forward to seeing more detail in the Annual Legislative and Work Programme on the Commission's proposals for improving access to justice.**

38.   The Minister, giving evidence before the Irish referendum, considered that the Commission's work in the area of freedom, security and justice during 2009 would be significantly affected by the entry into force of the Lisbon Treaty. He thought that there would not be a substantial number of new justice and home affairs proposals brought forward in the first few months after the Treaty's implementation, as the new architecture bedded down (Q 25). He considered that "a lot of the energy and time over the next few years on justice and home affairs issues will be about taking existing policies from Pillar Three governance and transposing them into the Community framework." The transposition of 82 Third Pillar measures into Community measures was "the substantial job that has to be completed over the next few years" (Q 26) and it would "limit the scope for additional initiatives in this field for some time to come" (p 10). The UK would have the right to choose whether to participate in (or opt in to) each of those measures as they were transposed.

39.   Clearly, the Irish "no" will have an impact on work in the area of criminal justice in 2009. Transposing existing Third Pillar measures into Community legislation cannot be undertaken unless or until the Lisbon Treaty is ratified by all 27 Member States. **We therefore encourage the Commission to press on in 2009 with initiatives envisaged under the Hague Programme and to work with the Council and the European Parliament to conclude measures currently under negotiation, such as the proposal on the application of the principle of mutual recognition to supervision orders in pre-trial procedures in the Member States.**

"Europe as a World Partner"

40.   The Commission's fifth priority is "consolidating the role of Europe as a global partner" (Q 34).[40] The Commission states in the Annual Policy Strategy that "[e]nergy security, climate change and migration will remain important guiding themes in external policy".[41] We note that these themes have been endorsed in European Council conclusions.

41.   The Commission says that in 2009, the European Neighbourhood Policy will focus on full implementation of the twelve European Neighbourhood Policy Action Plans.[42] The European Neighbourhood Policy was developed in 2004, with the objective of avoiding the emergence of new dividing lines between the enlarged EU and its neighbours, and instead strengthening the prosperity, stability and security of all states concerned. The central element of the European Neighbourhood Policy is the bilateral European

---

[40] Annual Policy Strategy pp 6–7

[41] Annual Policy Strategy p 6

[42] Annual Policy Strategy p 6

Neighbourhood Policy Action Plans, agreed between the EU and each partner. These set out an agenda of political and economic reforms with short and medium-term priorities. **We have some doubts about whether the "full implementation of the twelve action plans" in 2009 is a realistic ambition, but we encourage the Commission to make all possible progress.**[43]

42.   With regard to enlargement, the Commissioner told us that the Commission has "no intention" of changing its "very clear and strong commitments" towards Croatia and Turkey (Q 52) in the light of the Irish referendum.[44] She discussed the need to explain the "overwhelming" benefits of enlargement and how enlargement "has helped both development in the countries where [migrants] have come from and the countries in which they very often work", and added that thus far "[w]e have not been able to explain well enough the benefits of enlargement" (Q 60). **We welcome the Commission's continuing commitment to accession negotiations and the Copenhagen criteria.**

43.   Our Foreign Affairs, Defence and Development Policy Sub-Committee, Sub-Committee C, is conducting an inquiry into the European Security Strategy, adopted in 2003. There is no reference to the 2003 Strategy in the Annual Policy Strategy (nor to the security-development nexus[45]—see QQ 63–4). According to the Commission, this is because an improved and complemented European Security Strategy is scheduled for adoption at the end of 2008 (p 18); **we hope it subsequently becomes a priority for the Commission.**

---

[43] Annual Policy Strategy p 6

[44] Annual Policy Strategy p 6

[45] The security-development nexus reflects a wide international consensus that security and development are inextricably linked and mutually dependent. This consensus was notably expressed in the outcome documents of the international summit on United Nations reform in 2005.

CHAPTER 5: DELIVERY ON PROMISES: BETTER REGULATION

44. The Minister highlighted better regulation as one of the Government's top priorities out of those listed by the Commission (Q 3). The better regulation agenda at the EU level seeks to ensure that legislation is cost-effective and that it meets its stated objectives without imposing disproportionate burdens on public authorities and/or private operators. **The fact that "Better Regulation—Delivery on Promises and Change of Regulatory Culture" is one of the Commission's priorities for 2009, and features prominently in the APS, is welcome.**[46]

45. The Annual Policy Strategy states that "Better regulation is ... a key component of the EU's response to globalisation". The Commission says that it will take the lead in its efforts to improve the regulatory environment, and in developing high standards in areas such as health, safety and protection of the environment, to help shape global regulation.[47] The Commissioner told us that the Commission has "already integrated better regulation into our daily work in the [Directorates General] as part of our political priorities" (Q 44). In 2009 the Commission will continue to look for new simplification potential through the screening of the existing body of legislation, implementation of the Action Programme to reduce Administrative Burdens will be reviewed and progress in meeting the 25% reduction target for 2012 will be assessed (p 14). While the Annual Policy Strategy states that the Commission "intends to present a substantial number of proposals in 2009 designed to reduce administrative burdens", no detail about these proposals is provided in the Annex.[48] **It is encouraging that the Commission seems to be integrating better regulation more thoroughly into its work, and we look forward to seeing the detail of the Commission's proposals for reducing administrative burdens in the Annual Legislative and Work Programme.**

46. The Minister for Europe told us that in his opinion "the European Commission is making progress on better regulation" (Q 21), which we find encouraging. He added: "They have made, from a very low base ... progress, but not enough yet. With this Commission, from the President downwards, there is a determination to make progress but ... the Commission is a reflection on occasion of the demands of Member States and the 'something must be done' tendency ... Now on occasion nothing should be done" (Q 24). **We urge the new Commission which will begin its term in 2009 to build on the work of the Barroso Commission by mainstreaming better regulation principles in all its work and by resisting the "something must be done" tendency. The Commission intends to propose that its successor undertakes the exercise of testing proposals for legislation against better regulation principles and withdrawing many of them (p 14): this would be welcome, and we consider that all of the European institutions have a role to play in ensuring that the EU improves its regulatory performance consistently.**

47. We welcome the Minister's statement that "the United Kingdom government, along with a number of other Member States, is genuinely

---

[46] Annual Policy Strategy pp 7–8

[47] Annual Policy Strategy pp 7–8

[48] Annual Policy Strategy p 7

passionate about this … a better regulation agenda helps United Kingdom plc achieve so much else and can help Europe as well achieve so much more" (Q 22).

48. The Minister told us that the Commission's "consultation has to be wider: it has to consult small businesses much more effectively" (Q 21); we agree. **We urge the Commission to work towards drafting better EU legislation in its priority areas through improving its consultation of citizens and small businesses.** This should also contribute to the Commission's objective of "Communicating Europe".

49. The Commissioner told us that the Commission will continue to strengthen its impact assessment system in 2009 (p 14). **We congratulate the Commission on the increasing level of impact assessment of proposed legislation.** However, the Minister commented that the Commission "has to ensure that impact assessments are the norm" (Q 21). **Impact assessment should become standard practice for all proposals. In particular, the level of impact assessment of European Parliament and Council amendments should be increased.**[49]

50. The Minister told us that the Commission has to "have post-implementation assessments of the accuracy of the impact assessments because … these things gain by being revisited after three or five years to see whether they were accurate predictions, because one can never make a judgment as to whether these predictions are worth investing political capital in and whether they are accurate" (Q 21). **We agree: an evaluation of the accuracy of the impact assessment should be undertaken two to five years after each piece of legislation is adopted.**

51. **We also agree with the Minister's suggestion of including financial implications in the Commission's impact assessments (Q 21), and we urge the Commission to work on this suggestion.**

---

[49] See European Union Committee, 22nd Report (2007–08): *Initiation of EU Legislation* (HL 15), paras 62–63, 156.

CHAPTER 6: "COMMUNICATING EUROPE"

52. The Commission's section on its communication priorities for 2009 begins: "2009 will be a particularly important year for communicating Europe".[50] The Minister told us, "an awful lot of energy and some resource has been invested in this challenge … with limited success … but that is no reason to stop trying" (Q 10). **We emphatically agree.**

53. The Commission lists the communication priorities for 2009 as the Lisbon Treaty (particularly better governance and policies, the EU's role in the world, the area of justice, freedom and security, and the social dimension of the Charter of Fundamental Rights), budget reform, growth and jobs, and energy and climate change.[51] **We welcome the Commission's intention of prioritising just four communication themes. The Commission will need to give serious consideration to how it approaches this communication, and we look forward to seeing more detail on the Commission's plans in the Annual Legislative and Work Programme.**

54. The Commission says that communication priorities will "concentrate on areas of direct interest to EU citizens".[52] The Minister told us: "I do not believe that the disconnect with citizens is structural but largely about relevance, and until you have proved beyond doubt its contemporary relevance to the lives of citizens then euroscepticism will be alive and kicking in the United Kingdom and elsewhere, so it is essential that we have a sensible approach to localism, whether it is in technology, in democratic control or whatever" (Q 9). **The best way to interest citizens in Europe is by achieving and publicising results that are relevant to their lives and delivered locally, so we welcome the Commission's decision to concentrate communication on areas of direct interest to EU citizens.**

55. The likelihood is that the Lisbon Treaty will not enter into force at the beginning of 2009, and therefore the Commission's communication priorities are likely to change. We urge the Commission to keep its focus on areas of direct interest to citizens nonetheless. The Minister said, prior to the referendum, that "as we stop talking about structures and concentrate more on substance in the next few months and years I think we stand a much better chance [of engaging European citizens]" (Q 10), and **we hope that, whatever institutional debates take place in 2009, the focus on substance and on meaningful engagement will be maintained.**

56. The Commission's message on growth and jobs will be "presented in the perspective of citizens' concerns, including the European year for creativity and innovation."[53] Sub-Committee G has scrutinised the proposal and concluded that it had "considerable doubts that the European Year of Creativity proposed will add much of value to existing UK programmes", and concerns about the potential for the Year to divert resources from planned activities.[54]

---

[50] Annual Policy Strategy p 8

[51] Annual Policy Strategy p 8

[52] Annual Policy Strategy p 8

[53] Annual Policy Strategy p 8; Proposal for a Decision of the European Parliament and of the Council concerning the European Year of Creativity and Innovation (2009) (COM(2008) 159), 28 March 2008.

[54] Letter from Lord Grenfell to Bill Rammell Esq MP, Minister for life-long learning, dated 2 May 2008.

CHAPTER 7: HUMAN AND FINANCIAL RESOURCES

Human resources

57. The Commission will complete the phasing-in of additional staff needed due to the accession of Bulgaria and Romania in 2009, with the creation of 250 new posts.[55] Following this, the Commission has committed to meet all staffing needs by internal redeployment until 2013. 600 staff will be redeployed in 2009, with the 850 resulting posts "deployed to support the priorities set out in this Annual Policy Strategy, such as the Lisbon strategy for growth and jobs, implementation of the *acquis*, climate change and energy, and migration".[56] **We welcome this underpinning of APS priorities with real resources.** We note that the Commission is not requesting more staff for 2009 (as it did for 2008), and that it is requiring rationalisation in its Directorates General and services. **We also welcome the Commission's work on inter-institutional cooperation to make the most efficient use of resources.**[57]

The budget review

58. The Commission refers in the Annual Policy Strategy to the ongoing work on the budget review (ahead of the production of the Financial Perspective for 2014–2020). When asked whether the Government favoured "getting the Commission to pledge itself to revisit budget lines on the basis of zero-based budgeting periodically", and to reviewing budget lines which may have outlived their utility, the Minister replied: "that is generally much of the approach the United Kingdom is going to take on this comprehensive review of the budget in advance of the next financial seven year perspective" (Q 28). He added that the Government's principles for a modern budget are that the EU should act only where there is clear "EU added value", that EU action should be proportionate and flexible, recognising that expenditure is just one of a number of policy levers, that the full range of financing options (including grant and loan finance) should be considered, and that sound financial management and budget discipline should be adhered to (pp 10–11).[58]

The Commission's allocation of financial resources in the Annual Policy Strategy

59. Each year, the Commission's statements on changes in the allocation of financial resources in the Annual Policy Strategy anticipate the publication of the Commission's Preliminary Draft Budget, in which the Commission puts forward its spending proposals for consideration by the Council and European Parliament.[59] The figures in the Preliminary Draft Budget for 2009 differ from those in the Annual Policy Strategy, but not significantly. The

---

[55] Annual Policy Strategy p 9

[56] Annual Policy Strategy p 9

[57] Annual Policy Strategy p 9

[58] Subsequent to the Minister's evidence, the Treasury published *Global Europe: vision for a 21st century budget*, which expands on these principles (http://www.hm-treasury.gov.uk/media/2/2/global_europe190608.pdf). For this Committee's response to the budget review consultation, submitted in April, see European Union Committee, 18th Report (2007–08): *The 2009 EC Budget* (HL 140).

[59] Annual Policy Strategy pp 9–12

Preliminary Draft Budget has been scrutinised in detail by our Economic and Financial Affairs Sub-Committee, Sub-Committee A, but we here comment on whether the Commission seems to be backing up its priorities in the Annual Policy Strategy with financial resources.[60]

60. The Commission in its Annual Policy Strategy looked forward to requesting in the Preliminary Draft Budget an increase of €619 million (5.8%) for the budget sub-heading "Competitiveness for growth and employment", with the money going particularly to the Lisbon Strategy goals of competitiveness, sustainable growth and employment.[61] According to the Commission's proposals, funds would also be directed towards GALILEO and the European Institute of Innovation and Technology, the European Electronic Communications Market Authority, the Agency for the Cooperation of Energy Regulators, and preparatory action for Global Monitoring for Environment and Security operational services. More financial resources (an increase of €1,538 million, 2.5%) would also be channelled to the budget sub-heading "Cohesion for growth and employment". Details on these budget sub-headings were provided in the Commission's written evidence (pp 18–19). **While the Lisbon Strategy, GALILEO, and the EIT are all mentioned in the Commission's priorities, and Global Monitoring for Environment and Security services in the Commission's key actions, the Electronic Communications Market Authority and the Agency for the Cooperation of Energy Regulators are not discussed beyond the financial allocation section. We are not persuaded that the proposals for the Electronic Communications Market Authority are necessary.[62] We believe that the new agency is likely to increase regulatory complexity and bring insufficient benefits for the costs involved.**

61. According to the Commission's plan, under the budget heading "Preservation and management of natural resources" funds would be devoted to improved competitiveness of agriculture, better environment in rural areas, enhanced quality of life and diversification of the economy in the countryside.[63] More resources would also go to LIFE+ (the EU's financial instrument supporting environmental and nature conservation projects). In the Preliminary Draft Budget, an increase of €1,966 million (3.5%) is requested for this budget heading. **The relationship between this financial allocation and the Commission's priority of climate change and a sustainable Europe, focussing on energy, sustainable consumption, biodiversity, environmental law, maritime policy and the Common Agricultural Policy is not obvious.** The Commission's written evidence highlights the money going to the title "Environment and sustainable management of natural resources, including energy" in line with the Bali Roadmap, which is listed under the "Europe as a global partner" heading (pp 15–16) (see below).

62. The Annual Policy Strategy foresaw an increase of about €100 million (16%) for the sub-heading "Freedom, security and justice", with large allocations of additional funding going to external borders, visa policy, free movement of

---

[60] See European Union Committee, 18th Report (2007–08): *The 2009 EC Budget* (HL 140).

[61] Annual Policy Strategy pp 9–10

[62] See European Union Committee, 5th Report (2007–08): *The Single Market: Wallflower or Dancing Partner?* (HL 36).

[63] Annual Policy Strategy p 10

people, and common immigration and asylum policies.[64] More money would also go to the FRONTEX Agency, the European border surveillance system, the establishment of an entry-exit system and measures to facilitate travel at the external borders.[65] **This financial allocation matches the Commission's focus on immigration. However, although the Commission and the Government support measures to improve access to justice for citizens[66], it would appear that no specific financial support has been allocated to future projects in this area, which is disappointing. We hope that, notwithstanding the lack of earmarked funding, the Commission will propose specific projects including financial support to improve access to justice in cross-border cases, such as funding for video-conferencing, translators and action related to e-justice.**

63.   The Commission's statements on financial resource allocation envisage savings of €20 million for large-scale IT systems (SIS II, VIS and Eurodac) in 2009.[67] We asked the Commissioner how these savings would be realised. She said that since financial programming in 2005 the position had changed: "[c]ertain actions initially foreseen in 2009 will not be carried out as they are not on the political agenda and/or no legal basis is available (passport database, various studies, and projects in the domain of border management)", while the cost of the development of the Biometric component of the VIS (Visa Information System) had fallen (p 18).

64.   The Commission stated in the Annual Policy Strategy that around €630 million was earmarked for the budget heading "Citizenship", and indicated that this amounts to an increase of 5.3%.[68] The Commission said that this would allow more funding for key actions including public health, consumer protection, civil protection, cultural programmes and communication. **The Commission gives little detail here, but this allocation appears to be congruent with the Commission's priorities under "Putting the Citizen First". We would welcome more detail in the Annual Legislative and Work Programme on the ways in which the Commission's commitment to "Putting the Citizen First" will be translated into practical action backed by adequate funding.**

65.   Regarding the budget heading "EU as a global partner", the Commission described its prioritisation of the Middle East peace process and the implementation of the future status settlement of Kosovo.[69] While the Commission committed to increasing the amounts planned for Palestine and Kosovo, it said that the amounts will depend on developments in 2008 so it would fine-tune its requests during the budgetary procedure. The Commission noted that it would request €243 million in the 2009 Preliminary Draft Budget for the Common Foreign and Security Policy: while this is an increase of 21% on its request for 2008, it is actually 15% smaller than the amount finally allocated to this heading in the 2008 agreed

---

[64]   Annual Policy Strategy pp 10–11

[65]   See European Union Committee, 9th Report (2007–08): *FRONTEX: the EU external borders agency* (HL 60).

[66]   Annual Policy Strategy p 5; see the Government's Explanatory Memorandum on the Annual Policy Strategy for 2009 at http://europeanmemorandum.cabinetoffice.gov.uk/memo_details.aspx?memoID=1207

[67]   Annual Policy Strategy p 11

[68]   Annual Policy Strategy p 11

[69]   Annual Policy Strategy pp 11–12

budget. Assistance for the new EU strategy on Central Asia would be frontloaded in 2009 and 2010, and more money would go to the title "Environment and sustainable management of natural resources, including energy" in line with the Bali Roadmap. **It is not easy to see a close connection between the Commission's priorities for "Europe as a World Partner" and the financial allocation for external affairs, although this may be explained by the fact that part of the funding for external affairs is not distributed through the budget.** For example the European Development Fund, which is the main instrument for providing Community aid for development cooperation in the African, Caribbean and Pacific states and the Overseas Countries and Territories, does not come under the Community budget. It is funded by the Member States, subject to its own financial rules and managed by a specific committee.

CHAPTER 8: THE ANNUAL POLICY STRATEGY AS A CONSULTATION DOCUMENT

Our recommendations on the Annual Policy Strategy for 2008

66. In our report on the Annual Policy Strategy for 2008, we made a number of recommendations for improving the Annual Policy Strategy as a consultation document.[70] The Commission responded to our points in a letter from Commissioner Wallström of 28 September 2007.[71]

BOX 1

Recommendations on the Annual Policy Strategy for 2008, with Commission comments

Annual Policy Strategies should be more strategic. They should:

- Focus on only a few strategic goals, and provide the clear overarching strategy of the Commission's vision for the coming year;

- Be constructed from the top down, rather than succumbing to a Christmas tree tendency (having unnecessary material added to it in an unstrategic way);

- Provoke a constructive debate within and between the European institutions and national parliaments about the Union's priorities, by presenting the Commission's strategic thinking to the other institutions;

- Have the degree of clarity needed to form part of the Commission's efforts to increase public engagement.

  - *The Commission told us that it "agrees with the principle that the APS should as far as possible be focused on strategic priorities and provide a vision for the coming year", and defended the process currently in place to prepare the document.*

Annual Policy Strategies should give more explanation. They should:

- Be clearer about the specific status of each of the priorities or proposals listed;

- Include more background to the proposals so that the reader can more easily understand whether, in including a particular point, the Commission is prioritising a long-standing objective, re-affirming or updating such an objective, or tabling an entirely new initiative;

- Explain which policy areas have moved up the agenda in the past year (as well as which have moved down) and how the Commission's thinking has developed;

- Provide a clear justification for the key proposals, explaining the case for Union action and the limits on such action;

- Explain the added value of proposals, how they fit into the Commission's strategy and financial framework and how the Commission will ensure delivery of them.

---

[70] European Union Committee, 23rd Report (2006–07): *The Commission's Annual Policy Strategy for 2008* (HL 123).

[71] Published in Annex 3.

> - *The Commission thought that "[g]iving a justification, explaining the added value and discussing financial implications of each individual policy proposal in the APS would ... make the document rather difficult to read and would most likely change the character from a vision document to a rather detailed list of policy initiatives".*
>
> - *The Commission disagreed that the APS could be more strategic and also give more detail on the Commission's proposals, saying that "Being more specific or detailed on individual policy proposals at such an early stage is difficult, not least since the Commission is fully committed to respect our better regulation agenda including proper consultation and impact assessment on all initiatives ... A choice, therefore, has to be made and the Commission is clearly in favour of the more strategic approach".*
>
> Annual Policy Strategies should provide more financial detail. They should:
>
> - Explain clearly the financial constraints around the priorities, and the ways in which the Commission can (and cannot) change its spending priorities;
>
> - Match political priorities in budgetary terms, including by explaining which areas of funding are receiving less funding to allow the prioritisation of others;
>
> - Not include better regulation proposals, which should be published separately.
>
>   - *The Commission told us it "appreciates the need to explain more pedagogically in the APS the link between the APS and resources".*
>
> And Annual Policy Strategies should:
>
> - Discuss the EU's role in cross-cutting priorities where competence is shared with Member States, and how it interacts with Member States' action; and
>
> - Collect proposals under policy fields so that those looking at the Annual Policy Strategy can quickly find their areas of interest.
>
>   - *The Commission said that this "might facilitate a sectoral policy dialogue with other institutions", but "could lead the debate away from a more strategic vision", and it defended the inclusion of cross-cutting issues.*

2009: a better Annual Policy Strategy

67. In a number of ways the 2009 Annual Policy Strategy is a more readable document than that for 2008. The introduction is halved in length, and more focussed. While this partially reflects the nature of the coming year for the Commission, text looking back at the Commission's achievements has been cut out, which is welcome. The section outlining the Commission's priorities is much shorter. The lengthy listing of various disparate cross-cutting priorities is gone, which is an improvement. It is also helpful that the highlighting of (in the case of the 2008 Annual Policy Strategy) 39 sub-priorities has not been duplicated, which makes the Annual Policy Strategy at least appear more focussed.

68. The priorities themselves (such as "Making a Reality of the Common Immigration Policy") are more selective and specific. "Key actions" are relegated to an annex, rather than scattered amongst the priorities and sub-priorities, which again makes the Annual Policy Strategy look more strategic;

this distinction between priorities and delivery plans works better and foreshadows the Annual Legislative and Work Programme to come. Overall, **the Annual Policy Strategy for 2009 is more strategic, better organised, and looks less like a shopping-list than the Annual Policy Strategy for 2008.**

69.   We also recognise that the Commission has "a delicate balance to strike" between "the right level of detail" and allowing for "a proper political discussion on the priorities", especially given the breadth of the Union's activities (Q 60).

Scope for improvement: detail

70.   However, **we would encourage the Commission to go further in its improvement of the Annual Policy Strategy as a consultation document.** We believe that, in the context of a focussed strategy, **the Commission should include more explanation and justification of its priorities,** describing their added value and how they fit into the bigger picture of the EU's role. **The Commission should clearly describe which priorities or proposals are new and which are not, and what is moving up (or down) the Commission's agenda. The Commission needs to be clear about limitations as regards Union competence on some of its priorities (such as immigration).**[72]

71.   **The Commission's description of "Changes in the Allocation of Financial Resources", while a crucial part of the Annual Policy Strategy, is not readily comprehensible.** The Commission gives none of the context of the Annual Policy Strategy's financial allocation, and only those familiar with the intricacies of the EU budget process would understand this context and the Commission's references to budgetary headings and sub-headings. **The Commission's language is too specialised,** and there is no explanation of the meaning of "Initial programming", "APS changes" and "Revised programming" in the Commission's summary table.[73]

72.   **It is all but impossible, without reference to budget tables, to relate changes in financial allocations to the Commission's priorities.** The reader does not know which increases were long-scheduled and which relate to the Commission's decision to prioritise a particular policy area, and how these increases relate to the budgetary ceilings is also largely unclear. As a result, **it is difficult to decipher whether the Commission's financial allocations closely match their policy priorities, as well as to see where such a comparison is not relevant.** For example, it is not clear why the Electronic Communications Market Authority and the Agency for the Cooperation of Energy Regulators seem to be prioritised in the financial allocation but do not appear in the Commission's text. The reader should also be able to see clearly where funding for a particular policy will come from when it relates to a number of different budgetary headings, for

---

[72] As the Commissioner's written evidence to us points out, it is important that the Commission's policy initiatives are understood in the context that "they will always be only one part of the picture". "It is essential that all the actors in the EU's system of governance—the institutions, the Member States, public authorities at all levels—work together to convey more effectively the realities of the EU's objectives, actions and results" (p 13).

[73] Annual Policy Strategy p 13

example in the case of climate change work. **We would like to see greater correlation between the Annual Policy Strategy headings and the Preliminary Draft Budget, or more explanation of how they relate.**

73. We asked the Minister whether the Annual Policy Strategy should be costed in more detail. He replied: "It is essential that there is ... increasing attention paid to costings, of course ... it is essential the European Commission properly identifies a monetarised value of its proposals ... There is an improvement in the discipline of that but we are not where we should be." However, he added: "I am far from convinced that the APS is a way of doing that on the basis that the APS does not in itself contain the specific proposals, so I am not sure a monetarised assessment of the potential cost of general intention is the right way to go. The best way to capture that is when it gets to the status of specific legislative proposals and a monetarised value of a specific proposal" (Q 4).

74. We questioned the Minister on whether the Annual Policy Strategy matched the financial commitment made in the multi-annual Financial Perspective. The Minister said that the Annual Policy Strategy was important in terms of European Commission financing because it set a framework for the preliminary draft budget and could be seen as a guide towards the budget. But "the APS really does not claim to be, nor should it be seen as, a commitment of financial investment" (Q 5).

Scope for improvement: clarity of purpose

75. In our report on the 2008 Annual Policy Strategy, we concluded that **"future Annual Policy Strategies need to be clearer about the purpose of the document".**[74]

76. It was not clear to us whether the Annual Policy Strategy is written for the experts in the European institutions, or directed at European citizens. The Commissioner told us that it was meant for both, and that it was impossible to disconnect the institutional dialogue from "what we want to signal to the citizens" (QQ 35, 61). While we understand that the breadth of the Commission's work makes it difficult to narrow the Annual Policy Strategy down, and while we understand the temptation to advertise to the public its work on many diverse fronts, this will undermine the Strategy's communication function. **If the Commission wants the Annual Policy Strategy to provide citizens with a clear statement of the Commission's top priorities for the coming year, it will have to keep working on making the Annual Policy Strategy as focussed as possible and understandable to those without a detailed knowledge of the Union and its various programmes and policy dossiers. This would include the Commission further concentrating its priorities on a few issues that would be at the top of the public agenda, and easily understood by and communicated to the citizens.**

77. **However, it is important that the Annual Policy Strategy can perform its core function of sparking a useful dialogue between the institutions, Member States and national parliaments to shape the Annual Legislative and Work Programme.** The Commissioner said that

---

[74] European Union Committee, 23rd Report (2006–07): *The Commission's Annual Policy Strategy for 2008* (HL 123), p 9.

the Commission "attach great importance to this early dialogue on priorities for the upcoming year" (p 15). **If the Annual Policy Strategy cannot include enough detail to spark a useful dialogue between the institutions while remaining readable for the public, we suggest that the Commission focus the Annual Policy Strategy on this dialogue, and accompany it with a question-and-answer document or "citizens' summary" describing the Commission's top priorities (Q 62). This might be more profitable than focussing the Annual Policy Strategy on communication to citizens; as the Commissioner said, concrete actions are "what citizens will see, and very few ... will remember that as part of a five-point agenda" (Q 61).**

78.   After communication and consultation, the third effect of the Annual Policy Strategy is committing the Commission to action, which has a disciplinary function. The Minister told us that the Annual Policy Strategy is useful because it prevents people "decorating" the Commission with wish lists and "gives us a decent degree of guidance and a degree of predictability about the energy that is going to be invested over the subsequent twelve months" (QQ 2, 6). He said: "I would assume that, if an annual statement of this nature did not exist, then the conversation we would be having today is 'Why isn't there one?' It is important for all organisations to have a forward statement of their plan over the next 52 weeks" (Q 6).

The Government's treatment of the Annual Policy Strategy

79.   When we asked the Minister whether there was a proper dialogue on the Annual Policy Strategy between the Commission and the national governments and parliaments, he said, "I think there is" (Q 11). He told us that a response to the Annual Policy Strategy "impacts on the Commission's legislative work programme potentially ... the document in and of itself can be improved as Member States offer their reflections on it and as the European Parliament offers its reflections on it" (Q 18). He said that the Annual Policy Strategy itself is largely sourced indirectly from Council conclusions and commitments, so "the work in itself at its inception has taken account of the wishes of Member States and to a large extent often can reflect the concerns of national parliaments" (Q 12). The Commission explained the process of responding to national government concerns: "The Commission receives a response from Member States assembled in the Council of Ministers (comments from the 'Antici Group' composed of representatives of all Member States). The Commission systematically examines these contributions in the run-up to its Legislative and Work Programme which is presented in October each year and takes them into consideration when designing this Work Programme" (p 16).[75] **The Government should be making the most of this opportunity to influence the Commission's plans.**

80.   While the Minister said that the Annual Policy Strategy was "important", he was keen to emphasise that it was "useful in the context that it is a relatively internal document", and that we should not "overstate its significance, because in and of itself it does not create a single legislative vehicle" (Q 2). In its Explanatory Memorandum (EM) on the Annual Policy Strategy, the

---

[75] For an example of the Commission changing its policies in response to suggestions from Member States, see Q 54.

Government made only a few comments.[76] The Government stated that it welcomed the Annual Policy Strategy's publication; that it believed the Annual Policy Strategy should be "more readable and more focussed, with greater explanation of prioritisation of policy areas"; that it agreed with the Commission "that it is important that the EU focuses on delivering recognisable benefits and tangible policies that matter to its citizens"; that it "broadly" welcomed the Commission's policy priorities; that it believed "development should be recognised as an increasingly important part of Europe's role as a world partner"; and that it agreed that implementing the Global Approach to Migration remained a priority. **The Government's Explanatory Memorandum on the Annual Policy Strategy gives us the impression that the Annual Policy Strategy is not taken very seriously in Whitehall.**

81. **As we stated in our report on the 2008 Annual Policy Strategy, "our scrutiny and analysis of the APS needs to be assisted by a comprehensive Explanatory Memorandum from the Government."** [77]

82. Firstly, the Government needs to consult properly on its EM. The Minister told us how the Annual Policy Strategy is handled within Whitehall: "Cabinet Office ensures the distribution of the relevant material to Whitehall departments" (QQ 11, 18). **We recommend that the Government should ensure that the Annual Policy Strategy's financial allocations are seen and scrutinised by the Treasury, to inform both the EM and the Government's response to the Commission.**

83. When we asked the Minister whether devolved administrations were consulted on the Annual Policy Strategy, he commented: "there is an opportunity for devolved administrations through the Joint Ministerial Committee on Europe to play a role, but we should continue to find additional ways to make that more effective" (QQ 11, 30-31). He confirmed that the EM had been shared with the devolved administrations in March 2008 (p 10).

84. Secondly, as we urged in our report on the 2008 Annual Policy Strategy, **the EM "should present the Government's initial thoughts on [the Annual Policy Strategy's] proposals and priorities, and provide a preliminary assessment of the policy implications."** [78]

85. The EM stated that no fundamental rights issues applied, that the Annual Policy Strategy had no direct implications for subsidiarity, and that financial implications were not applicable.[79] When we questioned the Minister about the quality of the EM, he told us that it made no comment on fundamental rights issues "because the nature of the document is not a package of specific legislative proposals" (Q 25). The UK was "a primary advocate of the principle of subsidiarity", but "[s]ubsidiarity can only be considered on the basis of an individual proposal for legislation. Concerns cannot be inferred

---

[76] The Government's Explanatory Memorandum on the Annual Policy Strategy for 2009 is available at http://europeanmemorandum.cabinetoffice.gov.uk/memo_details.aspx?memoID=1207.

[77] European Union Committee, 23rd Report (2006–07): *The Commission's Annual Policy Strategy for 2008* (HL 123), para 55.

[78] European Union Committee, 23rd Report (2006–07): *The Commission's Annual Policy Strategy for 2008* (HL 123), para 55.

[79] See the Government's Explanatory Memorandum on the Annual Policy Strategy for 2009 at http://europeanmemorandum.cabinetoffice.gov.uk/memo_details.aspx?memoID=1207.

from the APS alone, and it is difficult to predict, ahead of seeing an individual draft proposal, whether or not the UK would have concerns with regards to subsidiarity" (p 10). **We consider that the Government should include in its EM its preliminary comments on proposals which may raise fundamental rights issues, which touch areas where subsidiarity may be a concern, and where significant financial implications will clearly arise.**

86. **In our view, there is a tension in the Government's attitude to the Annual Policy Strategy. Either the Annual Policy Strategy is an important statement of intent and provides a real opportunity for the European institutions, governments and parliaments to influence the Union's plans, or it is too vague for the Government to comment upon properly and is therefore not very useful or significant. If the former, the Government should be engaging fully with the Annual Policy Strategy and seeking to influence the Commission's priorities. It should be able to provide us with a detailed Explanatory Memorandum allowing us to scrutinise its positions, and in due course with its full response to the Commission. If the latter, the Government should be putting pressure on the Commission to make consultation on the Annual Policy Strategy a worthwhile exercise. Either way, the Annual Policy Strategy is the precursor to the Preliminary Draft Budget, and it would be extraordinary if the Government did not take a view on the allocation of financial resources the Commission proposes.**

CHAPTER 9: CONCLUSIONS

A year of changes at the top

87. We welcome the Commission's agenda of consolidation for 2009 as pragmatic. (para 7)

88. We think that the legislative lull in 2009 provides an excellent opportunity for the Commission to focus on the even-handed implementation of EU legislation across the Member States. That some of the 850 Commission posts to be newly created or redeployed in 2009 will be allocated to supporting the implementation of the *acquis* also reflects a welcome degree of commitment to this agenda. (para 8)

The Commission's priorities

89. We agree with the Commission's objective of delivering results on issues that concern citizens, and to communicate those results. The Commission's priorities should be based on the question of what makes the European Union relevant to the people of Europe. (para 10)

90. We welcome the priority on "Putting the Citizen First", but regret the lack of coherence among the disparate sub-priorities gathered underneath this heading. The Commission should do more to stress the weight it places on putting the citizen first throughout its work, thereby giving more coherence to this list of sub-priorities. Particular attention should be paid to issues impacting on communities and local projects. (para 11)

91. We welcome the Commission's focus on climate change, as crucial both to Europe's future and to connecting the EU with its citizens. Once the EU has agreed its package of energy and climate change measures, which it has agreed to do by early 2009 at the latest, the EU must strive for an environmentally and economically sustainable deal at the United Nations Climate Change Conference in Copenhagen in December 2009. (para 12)

92. The emphasis on "Europe as a World Partner" is also welcome, as the European Union must be in a position to address the challenges of a changing world in which China, India, Russia and other major powers and regions are rapidly playing a more important role. (para 13)

93. Delivering growth and jobs will also be fundamental to the role of the European Union in 2009, so we are glad to see it prioritised. (para 14)

94. The Commission's prioritisation of immigration reflects the importance most Member States attach to this issue and the priorities set by the Council. We welcome the collective efforts to tackle what is currently one of the major challenges facing the EU as a whole. We note, however, that the issue of immigration is far from uncontroversial for some Member States (particularly the United Kingdom, which has the right to choose whether to participate (the opt-in) in this area) and the Commission will need to handle this priority carefully, giving due regard to the principles of subsidiarity and proportionality and thereby showing that specific measures in this field add value. (para 15)

95. Given the critical importance of trade, the hazardous condition of World Trade Organisation negotiations and the rising protectionist threat in various

parts of the world, the Commission should make sure that trade is a priority for 2009. (para 16)

The details of the Annual Policy Strategy priorities

96. We encourage the Commission to keep up the momentum on the Lisbon Strategy. (para 17)

97. There will need to be careful consideration and case-by-case justification of any enhanced Commission role in international financial institutions. (para 20)

98. We look forward to seeing detail in the Annual Legislative and Work Programme about the ways in which the Commission will assist the European Institute for Innovation and Technology (EIT). We stress to the Government and the Commission the importance of ensuring the involvement of the private sector, most notably at the local level. (para 21)

99. We urge the Government to seek to ensure that the purpose of the EIT as a hub of innovation, without sucking up existing capacity and expertise, is followed in the development of the EIT. (para 22)

100. We are grateful for the Commission's clarification of the background to the proposed Communication on sectoral social dialogue and welcome it on that basis. (para 23)

101. We agree with the Government that the EU must not attempt to tackle the climate change challenge by applying protectionist measures. (para 24)

102. We note the Commission's efforts in the area of food and fuel prices, and urge the Commission, in their forthcoming work, to take into account changing views regarding the use of biofuels. (para 25)

103. The connected problems of high energy prices, energy security and climate change is exactly the sort of issue that the Commission needs to prioritise: where Member States are stronger together, and where it really matters to citizens. We encourage the Commission's efforts in this area and note the legislative initiatives it has undertaken to tackle climate change, and to reduce CO_2 emissions and dependence on oil by promoting the use of renewable sources of energy. (para 26)

104. We support the Government in its long-term ambition for fundamental CAP reform, and we urge the Commission to ensure that the Health Check agreement is implemented promptly and effectively in the course of 2009. (para 28)

105. We consider that the Commission's work on agricultural product quality must assist, rather than impede, progress towards improving the market orientation of the Common Agricultural Policy. (para 29)

106. A European Marine Observation and Data Network could be crucial in delivering an integrated marine policy and the Commission should concentrate on its careful design in order to ensure efficacy and avoid duplication of Member States' efforts. (para 30)

107. We support and encourage Commission initiatives to ensure that fisheries policy reflects the potential contribution that consumers can make in determining the sustainability or otherwise of EU fisheries, predominantly through clear, accurate and intelligible information provision. (para 32)

108. The implications of the Commission's initiatives on immigration need to be analysed and published for consultation before any legislative proposal is brought forward, along with the Commission's other impact assessment work focussing on the technical feasibility of these initiatives. Consideration is also needed as to whether any legislative proposals will meet the subsidiarity test and respect the proportionality principle. (para 33)

109. We endorse the shift of focus in the fight against terrorism to specific threats. (para 34)

110. Fundamental rights should have a more evident role in shaping policy. We would expect the Annual Policy Strategy, in discussing policies in areas affecting security and fundamental rights – such as immigration and criminal justice – to flag up human rights concerns and engage in a preliminary discussion of issues raised. (para 35)

111. While multiannual frameworks are important in the area of justice and home affairs, we would in future expect to see discussion in the Annual Policy Strategy, drawing on the multiannual framework, of the intended focus of the Commission's efforts in this field during the following year. We look forward to seeing more detail in the Annual Legislative and Work Programme on the Commission's proposals for improving access to justice. (para 37)

112. We encourage the Commission to press on in 2009 with initiatives envisaged under the Hague Programme and to work with the Council and the European Parliament to conclude measures currently under negotiation, such as the proposal on the application of the principle of mutual recognition to supervision orders in pre-trial procedures in the Member States. (para 39)

113. We have some doubts about whether the "full implementation of the twelve [European Neighbourhood Policy] action plans" in 2009 is a realistic ambition, but we encourage the Commission to make all possible progress. (para 41)

114. We welcome the Commission's continuing commitment to accession negotiations and the Copenhagen criteria. (para 42)

115. We hope that the improved European Security Strategy becomes a priority for the Commission after its adoption at the end of 2008. (para 43)

Delivery on promises: Better Regulation

116. The fact that "Better Regulation—Delivery on Promises and Change of Regulatory Culture" is one of the Commission's priorities for 2009, and features prominently in the APS, is welcome. (para 44)

117. It is encouraging that the Commission seems to be integrating better regulation more thoroughly into its work, and we look forward to seeing the detail of the Commission's proposals for reducing administrative burdens in the Annual Legislative and Work Programme. (para 45)

118. We urge the new Commission which will begin its term in 2009 to build on the work of the Barroso Commission by mainstreaming better regulation principles in all its work and by resisting the "something must be done" tendency. (para 46)

119. The Commission intends to propose that its successor undertakes the exercise of testing proposals for legislation against better regulation principles and withdrawing many of them: this would be welcome, and we consider

that all of the European institutions have a role to play in ensuring that the EU improves its regulatory performance consistently. (para 46)

120. We urge the Commission to work towards drafting better EU legislation in its priority areas through improving its consultation of citizens and small businesses. (para 48)

121. We congratulate the Commission on the increasing level of impact assessment of proposed legislation. (para 49)

122. Impact assessment should become standard practice for all proposals. In particular, the level of impact assessment of European Parliament and Council amendments should be increased. (para 49)

123. An evaluation of the accuracy of the impact assessment should be undertaken two to five years after each piece of legislation is adopted. (para 50)

124. We agree with the Minister's suggestion of including financial implications in the Commission's impact assessments, and we urge the Commission to work on this suggestion. (para 51)

"Communicating Europe"

125. We emphatically agree that 2009 will be a particularly important year for communicating Europe. (para 52)

126. We welcome the Commission's intention of prioritising just four communication themes. The Commission will need to give serious consideration to how it approaches this communication, and we look forward to seeing more detail on the Commission's plans in the Annual Legislative and Work Programme. (para 53)

127. The best way to interest citizens in Europe is by achieving and publicising results that are relevant to their lives and delivered locally, so we welcome the Commission's decision to concentrate communication on areas of direct interest to EU citizens. (para 54)

128. We hope that, whatever institutional debates take place in 2009, the focus on substance and on meaningful engagement will be maintained. (para 55)

Human and financial resources

129. We welcome the Commission's underpinning of Annual Policy Strategy priorities with human resources. We also welcome the Commission's work on inter-institutional cooperation to make the most efficient use of resources. (para 57)

130. While the Lisbon Strategy, GALILEO, and the EIT are all mentioned in the Commission's priorities, and Global Monitoring for Environment and Security services in the Commission's key actions, the Electronic Communications Market Authority and the Agency for the Cooperation of Energy Regulators are not discussed beyond the financial allocation section. We are not persuaded that the proposals for the Electronic Communications Market Authority are necessary. We believe that the new agency is likely to increase regulatory complexity and bring insufficient benefits for the costs involved. (para 60)

131. The relationship between the financial allocation for "Preservation and management of natural resources" and the Commission's priority of climate

change and a sustainable Europe, focussing on energy, sustainable consumption, biodiversity, environmental law, maritime policy and the Common Agricultural Policy is not obvious. (para 61)

132. The financial allocation for "Freedom, security and justice" matches the Commission's focus on immigration. However, although the Commission and the Government support measures to improve access to justice for citizens, it would appear that no specific financial support has been allocated to future projects in this area, which is disappointing. We hope that, notwithstanding the lack of earmarked funding, the Commission will propose specific projects including financial support to improve access to justice in cross-border cases, such as funding for video-conferencing, translators and action related to e-justice. (para 62)

133. The Commission gives little detail on the financial allocation for "Citizenship", but this allocation appears to be congruent with the Commission's priorities under "Putting the Citizen First". We would welcome more detail in the Annual Legislative and Work Programme on the ways in which the Commission's commitment to "Putting the Citizen First" will be translated into practical action backed by adequate funding. (para 64)

134. It is not easy to see a close connection between the Commission's priorities for "Europe as a World Partner" and the financial allocation for external affairs, although this may be explained by the fact that part of the funding for external affairs is not distributed through the budget. (para 65)

The Annual Policy Strategy as a consultation document

135. The Annual Policy Strategy for 2009 is more strategic, better organised, and looks less like a shopping-list than the Annual Policy Strategy for 2008. (para 68)

136. We would encourage the Commission to go further in its improvement of the Annual Policy Strategy as a consultation document. The Commission should include more explanation and justification of its priorities. The Commission should clearly describe which priorities or proposals are new and which are not, and what is moving up (or down) the Commission's agenda. The Commission needs to be clear about limitations as regards Union competence on some of its priorities (such as immigration). (para 70)

137. The Commission's description of "Changes in the Allocation of Financial Resources", while a crucial part of the Annual Policy Strategy, is not readily comprehensible. The Commission's language is too specialised. (para 71)

138. It is all but impossible, without reference to budget tables, to relate changes in financial allocations to the Commission's priorities. It is difficult to decipher whether the Commission's financial allocations closely match their policy priorities, as well as to see where such a comparison is not relevant. We would like to see greater correlation between the Annual Policy Strategy headings and the Preliminary Draft Budget, or more explanation of how they relate. (para 72)

139. Future Annual Policy Strategies need to be clearer about the purpose of the document. (para 75)

140. If the Commission wants the Annual Policy Strategy to provide citizens with a clear statement of the Commission's top priorities for the coming year, it will have to keep working on making the Annual Policy Strategy as focussed

as possible and understandable to those without a detailed knowledge of the Union and its various programmes and policy dossiers. This would include the Commission further concentrating its priorities on a few issues that would be at the top of the public agenda, and easily understood by and communicated to the citizens. (para 76)

141. However, it is important that the Annual Policy Strategy can perform its core function of sparking a useful dialogue between the institutions, Member States and national parliaments to shape the Annual Legislative and Work Programme. If the Annual Policy Strategy cannot include enough detail to spark a useful dialogue between the institutions while remaining readable for the public, we suggest that the Commission focus the Annual Policy Strategy on this dialogue, and accompany it with a question-and-answer document or "citizens' summary" describing the Commission's top priorities. This might be more profitable than focussing the Annual Policy Strategy on communication to citizens; as the Commissioner said, concrete actions are "what citizens will see, and very few ... will remember that as part of a five-point agenda". (para 77)

142. The Government should be making the most of the opportunity the Annual Policy Strategy provides to influence the Commission's plans. (para 79)

143. The Government's Explanatory Memorandum (EM) on the Annual Policy Strategy gives us the impression that the Annual Policy Strategy is not taken very seriously in Whitehall. (para 80)

144. As we stated in our report on the 2008 Annual Policy Strategy, "our scrutiny and analysis of the APS needs to be assisted by a comprehensive Explanatory Memorandum from the Government." (para 81)

145. We recommend that the Government should ensure that the Annual Policy Strategy's financial allocations are seen and scrutinised by the Treasury, to inform both the EM and the Government's response to the Commission. (para 82)

146. The EM should present the Government's initial thoughts on the Annual Policy Strategy's proposals and priorities, and provide a preliminary assessment of the policy implications. (para 84)

147. We consider that the Government should include in its EM its preliminary comments on proposals which may raise fundamental rights issues, which touch areas where subsidiarity may be a concern, and where significant financial implications will clearly arise. (para 85)

148. In our view, there is a tension in the Government's attitude to the Annual Policy Strategy. Either the Annual Policy Strategy is an important statement of intent and provides a real opportunity for the European institutions, governments and parliaments to influence the Union's plans, or it is too vague for the Government to comment upon properly and is therefore not very useful or significant. If the former, the Government should be engaging fully with the Annual Policy Strategy and seeking to influence the Commission's priorities. It should be able to provide us with a detailed Explanatory Memorandum allowing us to scrutinise its positions, and in due course with its full response to the Commission. If the latter, the Government should be putting pressure on the Commission to make consultation on the Annual Policy Strategy a worthwhile exercise. Either way, the Annual Policy Strategy is the precursor to the Preliminary Draft Budget, and it would be extraordinary if the Government did not take a view on the allocation of financial resources the Commission proposes. (para 86)

APPENDIX 1: EUROPEAN UNION COMMITTEE LIST OF MEMBERS

The members of the Select Committee which conducted this inquiry were:

> Lord Blackwell
> Baroness Cohen of Pimlico
> Lord Dykes
> Lord Freeman
> Lord Grenfell (Chairman)
> Lord Harrison
> Baroness Howarth of Breckland
> Lord Jopling
> Lord Kerr of Kinlochard
> Lord Maclennan of Rogart
> Lord Mance
> Lord Plumb
> Lord Powell of Bayswater
> Lord Roper
> Lord Sewel
> Baroness Symons of Vernham Dean
> Lord Tomlinson
> Lord Wade of Chorlton
> Lord Wright of Richmond

Declaration of Interests

Lord Freeman

> *Chairman, Thales Holdings UK plc (and chairman or director of a number of wholly owned subsidiaries of Thales Holdings UK plc including pension trustee companies)*
> *Director, Thales SA*

Lord Jopling

> *Partner in farming business*

Lord Powell of Bayswater

> *Director, LVMH (Moet-Hennessy Louis Vuitton)*
> *Director, Schindler Holdings*
> *Director, Northern Trust Global Services*

Lord Kerr of Kinlochard

> *Deputy Chairman, Royal Dutch Shell plc*
> *Non-executive Director, Rio Tinto plc (and Rio Tinto Ltd in Australia)*
> *Non-executive Director, Scottish American Investment Trust Co Ltd*
> *Member of the Advisory Board, Scottish Power (Iberdrola) (18 December 2007)*
> *Chairman of Court and Council, Imperial College*

A full list of Members' interests can be found in the Register of Lords Interests:

http://www.publications.parliament.uk/pa/ld/ldreg.htm

APPENDIX 2: LIST OF WITNESSES

The following witnesses gave oral and written evidence:

Mr Jim Murphy MP, Minister for Europe

Commissioner Margot Wallström, Vice-President of the European Commission and Commissioner for Institutional Relations and Communication Strategy

APPENDIX 3: EUROPEAN COMMISSION RESPONSE TO THE EUROPEAN UNION SELECT COMMITTEE REPORT ON THE ANNUAL POLICY STRATEGY FOR 2008

COMMENTS OF THE EUROPEAN COMMISSION ON AN OPINION FROM THE HOUSE OF LORDS[80]

COM(2007)65 - ANNUAL POLICY STRATEGY FOR 2008[81]

The Commission welcomes the Report from the House of Lords EU Committee on the Commission's Annual Policy Strategy (APS) for 2008 as a constructive contribution in view of the preparation of the Commission's Legislative and Work Programme (CLWP) for 2008.

The Commission takes note of the many clear and constructive ideas outlined in the report as to how the structure and presentation of the APS could be improved to make it more strategic and to allow a more focused and timely policy dialogue with the European Parliament, the Council and national parliaments in preparation of the CLWP.

The Commission agrees with the principle that the APS should as far as possible be focused on strategic priorities and provide a vision for the coming year. Nevertheless, it sees some tension in the report between this recommendation and the wish for a more detailed description of individual policy initiatives in the APS. Being more specific or detailed on individual policy proposals at such an early stage is difficult, not least since the Commission is fully committed to respect our better regulation agenda including proper consultation and impact assessment on all initiatives appearing on the CLWP later on in the year (except Green Papers, social partner consultation documents and regular reports). A choice, therefore, has to be made and the Commission is clearly in favour of the more strategic approach.

Presenting the annual policy strategy according to traditional policy areas (rather than following the Commission's strategic objectives) might facilitate a sectoral policy dialogue with other institutions. At the same time, such an approach could lead the debate away from a more strategic vision by focusing on sector-specific interests instead. The Commission considers the inclusion of a number of cross-cutting issues a positive element which should give a clear idea of the Commission's overarching priorities while allowing for sectoral expertise to become engaged in the debate.

The Commission agrees with the Committee that the APS should be construed around a set of clear strategic priorities defined at the political level around which operational services should provide their contributions. This, in fact, reflects rather well the process that is currently in place to prepare the document.

Like the Committee, the Commission attaches great importance to a constructive and politically anchored scrutiny process by the European Parliament, and also welcomes input from national parliaments, in view of preparing the CLWP. Time-wise, however, the input provided by these institutions should reach the Commission in the first semester of the year for it to be adequately taken into account by the Commission in the preparation of the CLWP. For information, the Commission services start preparing their input for the CLWP already in June/July.

---

[80] HL Paper 123

[81] COM(2007) 65

Giving a justification, explaining the added value and discussing financial implications of each individual policy proposal in the APS would, the Commission believes, make the document rather difficult to read and would most likely change its character from a vision document to a rather detailed list of policy initiatives. Some of the disadvantages of such an approach are discussed above.

The Commission appreciates the need to explain more pedagogically in the APS the link between the APS and resources. The various initiatives proposed by the Commission in the APS for 2008 should be seen in the context of the very recently agreed spending programmes and political priorities that underpin the overall financial envelopes agreed for the 2007-2013 Multi-Annual Financial Framework (MFF) in the Inter-Institutional Agreement of 17 May 2006. In terms of financial resources, the MFF indeed remains the framework for the APS and it has been fully taken into account when drawing up the APS. Section 3.2 of the APS only proposes marginal adjustments to the MFF.

With respect to the budgetary implications of the APS on an annual basis, the Commission considers that budget and policy should be seen as complementary. The purpose of the APS is precisely to set the political framework in which the annual budget is to be established. However, the institutional framework of the EU is such that there is seldom a direct link between the policy initiatives undertaken in a given year and their related expense in that same year. For instance, the 2008 Budget will finance actions which flow from legislative proposals presented in previous years, which the co-legislators have approved in 2007 or earlier. By the same token, the legislative proposals put forward in 2008 will have almost no budgetary implications for 2008, but will come on stream at the earliest in 2009. Furthermore, many initiatives from the Commission have little or no costs to the EU budget at all, such as the legislative actions in the area of the internal market or the application of EU competition rules.

The Commission's simplification work is programmed within the multi-annual Rolling Simplification Programme which has a horizon of 2-3 years and is updated every year (see COM(2006) 690), normally at the same time as the presentation of the CLWP. This medium-term forward planning is public and allows the other institutions and stakeholders to comment on the Commission's simplification priorities.

Whilst the Commission's Annual Report on Better Lawmaking is focused on progress during the preceding year (including key developments at the inter-institutional level), the Commission regularly undertakes strategic reviews on better regulation, setting out its priorities and policy initiatives for the following years. Such strategic reviews were presented in March 2005 (COM(2005) 97) and November 2006 (COM(2006) 689). The next review is planned for early 2008.

Following an external review of the impact assessment system, carried out between August 2006 and April 2007, the Commission is currently reviewing its impact assessment methodology and guidelines. In this context, the Commission is examining how the assessment of particular aspects such as competitiveness, social impact, and fundamental rights can be reinforced without jeopardising the overall balanced and proportionate approach to impact assessment.

Concerning the sometimes detailed comments on individual policy initiatives in the APS provided by the sectoral sub-committees of the House of Lords, the Commission will consider these when it draws up its CLWP for 2008. The Commission will also communicate these comments to the competent services which may decide to take them into account when developing the policy initiatives further.

APPENDIX 4: RECENT REPORTS FROM THE SELECT COMMITTEE

Session 2007-08

Priorities of the European Union: evidence from the Minister for Europe and the Ambassador of Slovenia (11th Report, Session 2007–08, HL Paper 73)

The Treaty of Lisbon: an impact assessment (10th Report, Session 2007–08, HL Paper 62)

Session 2006–07

Evidence from the Minister for Europe on the Outcome of the December European Council (4th Report, Session 2006–07, HL Paper 31)

Government Responses: Session 2004–05 (6th Report, Session 2006–07, HL Paper 38)

The Commission's 2007 Legislative and Work Programme (7th Report, Session 2006–07, HL Paper 42)

Evidence from the Ambassador of the Federal Republic of Germany on the German Presidency (10th Report, Session 2006–07, HL Paper 56)

The Commission's Annual Policy Strategy for 2008 (23rd Report, Session 2006–07, HL Paper 123)

The Further Enlargement of the EU: follow-up Report (24th Report, Session 2006–07, HL Paper 125)

Evidence from the Minister for Europe on the June European Union Council and the 2007 Inter-Governmental Conference (28th Report, Session 2006–07, HL Paper 142)

EU Reform Treaty: work in progress (35th Report, Session 2006–07, HL Paper 180)

Remaining Government Responses Session 2004–05, Government Responses Session 2005–06 (37th Report, Session 2006–07, HL Paper 182)

Correspondence with Ministers January–September 2006 (40th Report, Session 2006–07, HL Paper 187)

Minutes of Evidence

TAKEN BEFORE THE SELECT COMMITTEE OF THE EUROPEAN UNION

TUESDAY 10 JUNE 2008

Present	Blackwell, L	Mance, L
	Cohen of Pimlico, B	Plumb, L
	Dykes, L	Roper, L
	Grenfell, L. (Chairman)	Sewel, L
	Harrison, L	Tomlinson, L
	Howarth of Breckland, B	Wade, L
	Jopling, L	Wright of Richmond, L
	Kerr of Kinlochard, L	

Examination of Witness

Witness: MR JIM MURPHY, a Member of the House of Commons, Minister for Europe, examined.

Q1 *Chairman:* Thank you very much, Minister, for being with us. We have just had an interesting hour with the Ambassador on the French Presidency priorities, so we are all fired up and ready to go now on the Annual Policy Strategy, moving forward from the second half of 2008 to what is going to happen in 2009. Do you want to make an opening statement?

Mr Murphy: I am happy to go straight into the questions.

Q2 *Chairman:* Maybe you would like to start by telling us what real value the Government puts on the APS? I thought that the Explanatory Memorandum was interesting but it said very little in terms of opinions and assessments of the value of it. It was a very good recital of what is in it, but at the end it was fairly brief on what you felt was the real value of it and what individual aspects of it appealed to the Government. Could you talk a little bit about what good you see in this exercise?

Mr Murphy: Of course; I will happily do so. What is important is to get a sense of really what purpose the document serves. As your Lordships will be aware, it is not a statement of legislative intent: it is a statement of intention. In that sense we consider it to be useful but it is useful in the context that it is a relatively internal document which gives us a decent degree of guidance and a degree of predictability about the energy that is going to be invested over the subsequent twelve months, so on that basis it is an important predictor of what is to follow, but that is all it is. It is not prescriptive: it probably is not as detailed as others would wish; but it certainly is more detailed than the multi annual strategic work plan, it is a bit more granular than that. On that basis it is important and useful but I do not think we should overstate its significance, because in and of itself it does not create a single legislative vehicle.

Q3 *Chairman:* There are seven priority actions mentioned by the Commission, so you are right in saying that this is not a legislative programme but a statement of intentions, which are fairly well defined. I am just probing a little bit to know what you see as the really high priorities from the Government's point of view, amongst those identified by the Commission as their priorities.

Mr Murphy: On the seven, climate change, not least for the geopolitical reasons and the impending argument about a global climate change, which is that if Europe either reneges on its commitment on renewables and other aspects of the climate change package or gives the impression of being luke warm I think it will send a signal to other groups of nations across the planet and would have a negative impact on other world capitals, not least in Brazil, Russia, Washington and elsewhere. There is a double pressure point to climate change, I think. Firstly, there is the pressure point about trying to get a global success at Kyoto but, secondly, and the French Ambassador may have spoken about this as the important one the French would like to see during their Presidency on climate change, the fact that after the French the Czechs will have the opportunity to assume the Presidency, and please, I know the Czech government would not take this as an implicit criticism so your Lordships should not take it as such either, but the jury is still out in Prague as to the need for a concerted effort on climate change, so if I were to say what the time pressure priority is it is important we make progress on climate change for one internal Europe reason and one much wider reason. Other than that, without going into detail, better regulation, and, thirdly, it is a watching brief on justice and home affairs. Now, I am not saying the others are not important, but if your Lordships ask me for some sort of hierarchy that would be my response this afternoon.

Q4 *Baroness Cohen of Pimlico:* My question is not on climate change but on the general question of tying the APS to budgets, because my sub-committee which looks at budgets rather yearns to see some of the APS' proposals costed or some kind of indication as to where the money will be coming from to render any of these policies possible in any way at all, or within any known timescale. Do you have any comments on the Commission's general framework for human and financial resources? There are very few. The Government's EM said that financial implications are not applicable to the APS. Well, shouldn't they be? Would we not be better off with a costed APS? How do you see it fitting into the system?

Mr Murphy: It is essential that there is, first, increasing attention paid to costings, of course. I am not certain the APS is the right vehicle to do that but it is essential the European Commission properly identifies a monetarised value of its proposals. This is absolutely essential. There is an improvement in the discipline of that but we are not where we should be. I am far from convinced that the APS is a way of doing that on the basis that the APS does not in itself contain the specific proposals, so I am not sure a monetarised assessment of the potential cost of general intention is the right way to go. The best way to capture that is when it gets to the status of specific legislative proposals and a monetarised value of a specific proposal, so in general, of course, you are right, there needs to be progress along the lines you have suggested, but I do not believe the APS is the most cost effective way of doing it on the basis that it is a relatively broad-ranging set of commitments rather than specifics.

Q5 *Lord Tomlinson:* Minister, one of the first things I always look at in government explanatory memoranda is the statement of financial implications, and I am always fascinated to see how great and wide the ambitions are and how usually the financial implications are stated as nil. In your Explanatory Memorandum on this you say that financial implications are not applicable to the APS but, as I look through some of the ambitions of it, I see 619 million euro for the Lisbon agenda, a specific 1,538,000,000 euro for cohesion for growth and employment, 16% more for freedom, security and justice. What kind of assurance can you give the Committee that the sort of general framework that is put before us in an annual policy strategy and the implication it has for human and financial resources for 2009 matches the financial commitments that have been made in the framework, in the annual budget, in the financial perspectives? How do they all match up? Or is the APS even a little bit less than you implied at the beginning and a total waste of time because it is financially incoherent?

Mr Murphy: Discuss! I do not believe it is irrelevant, far from it, but neither do I believe we should overstate its importance. That is the balance I am trying to strike in my comments thus far this afternoon. It does set a framework for the preliminary draft budget and I think that is the importance of the APS in terms of European Commission financing and, therefore, it is a guide towards the budget. Now, I have not had the opportunity, I do not believe, to share with your lordships Committee thinking on the budget, and I may be committing a different minister for that purpose and if that is what I am doing I apologise, but there may be an additional purpose in having a conversation about the preliminary draft budget and the fiscal consequences of that, because, returning to the point already raised, the APS really does not claim to be, nor should it be seen as, a commitment of financial investment, that is done through the preliminary draft budget, and it does not commit the Commission to spending.

Q6 *Lord Tomlinson:* So, really, is it anything more than a Christmas tree on which everybody hangs their wish list for presents?

Mr Murphy: I think it prevents the European Commission becoming a Christmas tree and enabling people to hang their presents, because normally it would be a year-long aspiration of work that is to be completed and for me what it does is it prevents in February, March, April—right up to Christmas— people decorating the Commission with a new wish list. So I think that is one of the things it prevents. It gives a degree of predictability: it is more granular in its detail than the multi annual work plan. I would assume that, if an annual statement of this nature did not exist, then the conversation we would be having today is "Why isn't there one?" It is important for all organisations to have a forward statement of their plan over the next 52 weeks, and that is really what it is, but that is all we should see it as.

Q7 *Lord Kerr of Kinlochard:* I agree with you, Minister, about its usefulness, but I do not think the Explanatory Memorandum can be said to be quite so useful. I agree with Lord Tomlinson. The second half of the strategy document is devoted to description of movements of money between different headings; and comparisons between the new totals and their breakdown, and the totals in the financial perspectives and their breakdown. It is not clear to me how that relates to the budget: it is not clear to me that the remaining headroom under the ceilings, which is spelled out, is sufficient; and that does seem to me to be a serious financial implication, which the Government might want to think about. In all cases, as I read it, and I may have got the numbers wrong, the available headroom is well under 1% of the money under that sub ceiling in the financial perspective. Now, I agree with you, this exercise probably does have the disciplinary effect inside the Brussels institutions, but it seems to me we ought for that very reason to take it seriously and see if we agree with the shifts that they are describing and in some cases proposing; the words "the Commission proposes" occur from time to time. What is our view of their proposals; and do we think the sum of the proposals comes sufficiently below the ceilings or rather close? In my personal view it is rather close, but I may be wrong.

Mr Murphy: On the specifics, on finance, without wishing to add too much to what I have already referred to, in the introduction to the APS it does talk about, if my recollection is right, increased staffing of 250 to deal with the final component of the enlargement regarding Bulgaria and Romania, and there are no further staffing commitments other than those which would be met by internal reprioritisation. I would not wish to disagree with the noble Lord's general financial point, but it may be helpful for your Lordships if, when it comes to the draft preliminary budget, I return, which I am happy to do, to have this specific conversation about the specific fiscal proposals.

Q8 *Lord Kerr of Kinlochard:* But some of this is presumably money being spent this year, and when it comes to the budget you are looking at the money for next year?

Mr Murphy: Yes. The way it would work is that the APS for 2009 would help inform the CLWP, the Commission's legislative work programme, which is published in final form in December. It is I think published initially in October with conversations and discussions in European capitals and parliaments in between October and December, with, alongside that, the preliminary budget. So it is a package of proposals for 2009. Individually each of the documents serve a specific purpose but together the three documents serve a combined aggregate function, which I think is about right.

Q9 *Baroness Howarth:* Following up this question but taking it into a slightly different area, one of the budgetary problems at the end of last year was the funding of the EIT and the question of finding money within the margins in order that the European Institute of Technology could be set up. Subsequently we asked a number of questions about whether or not that would affect the KICs, the local projects, in relation to developing small businesses and making sure that that work went on locally. I was assured at the COSAC meeting that that was so and that really the focus should be on local. Now, one of the objectives of next year's programme is to involve local citizens to make sure that Europe makes sense

to local citizens, and keeping things local does help with that. However, I have recently had sight of another document which describes where the funding for EIT is going to come from, and that includes a comment that it will come from local projects. Now, which local projects? That is another document we have for scrutiny, and the question of which local projects is difficult. But you see the confusion that arises if the project is not thought through in terms of the funding from the beginning because it affects the policy and whether the policy is to set up a huge institute, which we are assured it is not, or whether the policy is to have an institute that maintains and develops local and which feeds in, then, to helping Europe to become much more understood by local communities.

Mr Murphy: Again, there are three or four different aspects to the question, noble Lord Chairman. The purpose of the European Institute, in my understanding, is to be a European hub of innovation, it is not to create a research and development monster and it is not to suck up capacity and expertise that already exists in other European capitals, and not just in capitals but in different regions and towns and cities throughout the European Union. I have not had the option to read the document referred to but I am happy to do so, if you wish me to, and to reflect on it. In terms of the localism point, I share the assessment which I have referred to in debates on the Lisbon Treaty in the Commons about the problem with Europe in terms of the disconnect with citizens, and I do not want to talk about Ireland and the Lisbon Treaty, that is perhaps for another time. I do not believe the disconnect with citizens is structural but largely about relevance, and until you have proved beyond doubt its contemporary relevance to the lives of citizens then euro scepticism will be alive and kicking in the United Kingdom and elsewhere, so it is essential that we have a sensible approach to localism, whether it is in technology, in democratic control or whatever. So it is essential.

Q10 *Baroness Howarth:* You think it becomes more meaningful when people become engaged in that way?

Mr Murphy: It is more meaningful, and it is something that an enormous amount of energy is expended upon. My approach in these evidence sessions is to try and be entirely frank, and an awful lot of energy and some resource has been invested in this challenge, and I think, on fair reflection at the moment, with limited success. The opportunities for information technology and internet activism around the European Union have met with limited success, but that is no reason to stop trying, but as we stop talking about structures and concentrate more on substance in the next few months and years I think we stand a much better chance.

Q11 *Lord Roper:* I want to follow up something asked at the beginning, which concerns the process by which we are able to influence the APS. What action does the Government take to influence the Annual Policy Strategy, and are you satisfied with the system the Commission has in place for ensuring that the views of national governments and parliaments are taken into account? Is there a proper dialogue, and is it effective?

Mr Murphy: I think there is, but I have never sought to say that things cannot continue to evolve and improve. In terms of how to handle it across Whitehall and with devolved administrations, Cabinet Office ensures the distribution of the relevant material to Whitehall departments. I think within perhaps two or three separate ring rounds of Whitehall departments there is an opportunity for devolved administrations through the Joint Ministerial Committee on Europe to play a role, but we should continue to find additional ways to make that more effective. I am content the system at the moment works pretty effectively, but I am sure it could be improved upon.

Q12 *Lord Roper:* How is this fed into the Commission system, and are you satisfied that they take any notice of what anybody else says?

Mr Murphy: On the basis that the building blocks of the annual policy programme of work are largely sourced from the multi annual work plan which is largely sourced from Council conclusions and commitments, if you look at the building blocks that way you could argue that the work in itself at its inception has taken account of the wishes of Member States and to a large extent often can reflect the concerns of national parliaments, but, once you get to the final point, governments through the European Council and national parliaments have an opportunity to make their observations and then those are all brought together, and if amendments are needed to the annual work plan they can take place. So there is a myriad of different pressure points in the process, but the most effective pressure point is at the beginning to make sure, where we can, that the annual programme of work is rooted in the multi annual work plan, and that the multi annual work plan is a reflection of the wishes of Member States at the beginning.

Q13 *Lord Roper:* We as sub-committees and in this Committee put in a certain amount of time to consider this, and I suppose what we are really saying is what evidence do we have that this is a useful way of spending our time.

Mr Murphy: On occasion we all would reflect on that, and I think your Lordship's Committee and other Committees reflected on the impact that the House of Lords and Committee Reports in particular can have on the thinking in Brussels and in other European capitals. The most celebrated example, of course, is that of mobile phone telephony where undoubtedly the reflections of your Lordships had an impact not just on thinking but on action. That is the most celebrated example, and rightly so.

Q14 *Lord Roper:* We can see very clearly the cases of individual proposals but I am really thinking about the consideration of these very general documents, as to whether reports on them are a useful way for us to spend our time in terms of the way in which our reports are then used in the refinement of such a strategy.

Mr Murphy: I think they undoubtedly are reflections of your Lordship's Committee and other Committees of the House of Lords, and there is a debate we are having in the House of Commons on Thursday on this work in particular. The reflections that your Lordship's Committee offers on the multi annual programme of work and the Annual Policy Strategy are important, but also the way in which Her Majesty's Government feeds into this process is impacted upon by the observations of your Lordship's Committee and the Committee of the House of Commons on our ambitions on global Europe, so I would contend that again there is a myriad of pressure points. It is not the Government's job to invite additional pressure on the points but there are undoubtedly different ways in which you can influence this work, partly by reports that are read in other European capitals but in particular by continuing to pressure Her Majesty's Government on these issues.

Q15 *Chairman:* Can I follow up a little bit on what Lord Roper has been saying on this question to you? In paragraph 37 of the Explanatory Memorandum you express your disappointment that the APS is not more readable and more focused with greater explanation of prioritisation of policy areas. If they succeeded in doing something about that, and this is very much what we were saying when we did our report on how the APS was put together, if there was more prioritisation, would the Government then in an Explanatory Memorandum be prepared to be more forthcoming and tell us what they think of their priorities? At the moment you have said there is not any prioritisation, and it appears that seems to have let you off the hook of having to say yourselves what you think of what priorities you can unearth in this document?

Mr Murphy: I think this year forthcoming and 2009 is unusual in the same way that every five years there is an unusual year. The APS and possibly the Explanatory Memorandum—and I apologise to your Lordships if it turns out to be more impenetrable than is normally the case: it is not our intention and I will reflect on whether the Explanatory Memorandum cannot be improved in future, of course—is a reflection of the dynamic of the year we are about to approach. As the introduction to the document itself states, most of the substantial legislative proposals have already been tabled in 2008 and, therefore, we are in that period of every five years where there is, to be frank, a degree of uncertainty with the European elections and much else besides approaching us. I will reflect on whether the EM can be improved for future hearings and, of course, we should always try and make the Commission and the European Union as accessible as is possible, and this was a point made this morning. I hosted a seminar this morning at the Oval cricket ground about the European Union on sport, and this was a common frustration. For example, and I do not want to take us down a side track and your Lordship would chastise me for doing so, but take, for example, the nature of the word "specificity" in the context of sport; it is another one of those words that has its origins in the English language but which does not have a clear English meaning, like "flexicurity", so there are two words that are seemingly English in their origin but have no precise definition. So it is a continual challenge and I would be churlish to suggest there is an easy solution, but as a general principle, my Lord, you are, of course, correct.

Q16 *Chairman:* For "specificity" read "opt-out".
Mr Murphy: Well, that is one interpretation but specificity does not allow for opt-out on a free movement of labour, which obviously is an issue about UEFA who are saying that Arsenal should only have five foreign players, so specificity is not an opt-out because, while other European capitals misinterpret it or reinterpret it as an opt-out, the United Kingdom government will defend the fact that the free movement of labour applies to all professions across the European Union including sport, whether it is football or basketball or rugby.

Q17 *Lord Sewel:* Can I ask you really for your degree of optimism on making progress on two topics that appear in the APS? One is the health check and achieving a consensus and then implementing it, and I suppose there what is interesting is the extent to which France has really changed and the attitude it will bring to the Presidency at the time when it will be leading on the health check, and the second one is climate change and energy. The next twelve months are going to be very important and the lead-up to Copenhagen and developing a robust European position. My Lord Jopling and I, not wearing EU hats but NATO Parliamentary hats, recently were in Bulgaria and Romania looking very much at energy climate change issues and, really and truly, in those two countries, the response we got time and time again was concentration on energy security, yes, and price and cost, and when you tried to extend the argument into the link with the environment and CO_2 I am afraid you got pretty glazed looks. It was: "Well, we are poor countries, we cannot really afford that indulgence", which was a bit depressing. So I am wondering the extent to which you can get a real European-wide position in anticipation of Copenhagen when really there are separate discourses going on, even within Europe.
Mr Murphy: On the specific question of agriculture and whether France has changed, we will see! The Ambassador, of course, will have offered his government's observations, but the health check is important in terms of looking to simplify the single payment scheme and other farming and agricultural reforms, and it is also important, secondly, to have a conversation about the longer term. But we are very firm that the health check should not be used to set a longer term strategy on agricultural reform which is limited in its ambition. It has to be a wholesale reform of the Common Agricultural Policy, that is our starting point and it is where we wish to get to. There can be in a health check specific improvements but it is not a replacement for a wider reform of the Common Agricultural Policy. To be fair to the French I do not think that is what they see it as but I know there is a temptation in some European capitals for that to happen. In terms of climate security and energy, of all the issues that understandably excite public comment in the United Kingdom I think energy security is the one where the degree of strategic importance and public comment is most out of kilter. We talk about energy security and routes to market often through the prism of the posture of the Government in Moscow and it becomes more accessible in that context, but the viability and security of energy supply in a period where we are climate change sensitive and where the supply pressures exist in the dramatic way they do is one of the biggest strategic challenges in every country in the European Union and beyond. As for the solution, as your noble Lords are only too well aware, we are not in the position that China or Russia would be in. They have a single chequebook with a single pen. We do not. If we have a chequebook at all there are 27 hands and 27 pens, and we are not in the position where we can simply strike a deal in central Asia or elsewhere. So there is so much to this issue. I was in Azerbaijan last month meeting the President and we had conversations about routes to market and the Baku pipeline, there are issues about Ukraine and the

proposals to sign a neighbourhood agreement with Ukraine which would include the modernisation of their energy transmission networks, so there is so much to this, and the third part of the noble Lord's question then picks up the sentiment in other European capitals and beyond. It is not just in the developing nations that this conversation is pretty lively. If we look at the conversation in Paris and elsewhere there is this phrase "carbon leakage", another impenetrable phrase but on examination we know what it means—it is the fact that put colloquially why should we do the right thing when others will not? In doing the right thing the issue is not carbon leakage; it is the transfer of jobs as capital and investment opportunities move elsewhere with a less rigorous climate change regime. Now, this is a part of a continuing conversation but Her Majesty's Government is very strongly of the view that the solution to this is not a carbon tariff or a protectionist tariff of any sort, because it is pretty dangerous if the international message is that the only way you can do the right thing on climate change is by virtue of a new round of tariffs, and it would lead very quickly to retaliatory measures. So that is the debate not just in developing economies, which of course it is in a different point of their economic evolution, but it is also an important debate in Paris, and there is pressure in Berlin with the niche car industry in terms of the climate change package. That is why I started by saying what our priority is, and I mentioned climate change in the first place, because there are European pressures here which are pretty acute, and there are time limits concerning not only Copenhagen but the impending Czech Presidency as well, and that is why we need to make progress during the French Presidency.

Q18 *Lord Kerr of Kinlochard:* I think the Explanatory Memorandum is the sort of document the Foreign Office—a wonderful Department, by the way—writes extremely well; it is a descriptive document describing somebody else's plans. But they are not somebody else's plans, they are our plans, the Commission's money is our money, and the money bit at the back does give you a hint as to priorities, and there are statements in here that are very political. Do we agree that the current financial turmoil calls for a co-ordinated EU response "including a stronger presence of the Commission in international financial institutions"? I am not sure that I do; and that is quite a political statement by the Commission. So the policy implications bit at the back of our Explanatory Memorandum seems to me to be as inadequate as the financial implications bit, as Lord Tomlinson pointed out, and that is because, I suspect, this document is being treated as not very important. The sentence that I have just read out from the document is one that would, I imagine,

cause people in the Treasury to sit up and take notice. The only Treasury paragraph on this that I can see is the "financial resources" three sentence discussion of what is half the paper, and I guess that it was written—because it is beautifully written—not in the Treasury but in the Foreign Office! So it seems to me that we need to decide whether this is an interesting description of Commission plans which we do not need to bother about (in which case, if that is the Government's view, then maybe we need not bother so much about scrutiny of the document), or, whether it is an opportunity to influence thinking in the Commission, to tell them that we do not think their implicit priorities as demonstrated by the way they want to move money about are right, or to tell them when we do not agree with a statement they make. Maybe the Government does agree that we want to see a stronger presence of the Commission in the international financial institutions, in which case that in itself would be quite interesting.

Mr Murphy: I do not want to enter into open speculation as to which government department wrote which sentence of which paragraph, but the noble Lord, as always, has a degree of accuracy in what he is reflecting upon. In terms of the role of Europe in these international debates and international institutions, the Prime Minister himself invited leaders of France, Germany, Spain, Italy and the President of the Commission to Downing Street to discuss these very issues, so there is a role for the Commission, although the exact shape and nature of that role is open to conjecture and continued discussion. The Explanatory Memorandum is the Government's rather than any one government department's. I think the importance of this document, which I tried to allude to earlier, is that between now and October, when the Commission's legislative work programme is published, the response to this document, I would argue, impacts on the Commission's legislative work programme potentially, and to be frank that is one of the important aspects of evidence sessions such as this. So the document in and of itself can be improved as Member States offer their reflections on it and as the European Parliament offers its reflections on it, but the period between now and October before the Commission publishes—and we hope they stick to the timetable of October despite other pressures—is a point of maximum influence as a consequence of these hearings.

Chairman: Could I make one comment on the general framework of the Human and Financial Resources, which is Part II of the APS? I must say I was very pleased to see there is now a section "Changes in the Allocation of Financial Resources". Lord Tomlinson may correct me if I am wrong but I seem to remember that was a point we made very strongly with the Commission when we met because it was something that was missing from the previous one, so may we strike one for the European Union Select Committee in that we seem to have got across to the Commission that they should focus on changes to the allocation resources? Am I not right?

Lord Tomlinson: Absolutely, Lord Chairman. Your recollection, as ever, is totally immaculate!

Q19 *Lord Wade of Chorlton:* I would like to explore a little bit the Government's views on European regulation. We talk about "better regulation", et cetera, and I have not the slightest idea what the word "better" means in this context, but I would like to get a view of what government feels about it. Do you think there is an issue relating to continuing EU regulation? We know for a fact from evidence we have had that there are some concerns in some quarters. How do you feel you will react over the next twelve months to better regulation suggested in the agenda?

Mr Murphy: Unlike "specificity" I would argue a pretty clear understanding about what "better regulation" means.

Q20 *Lord Wade of Chorlton:* You tell me.

Mr Murphy: I think it is proportionate regulation—

Q21 *Lord Wade of Chorlton:* Proportionate to what?

Mr Murphy: —by which I mean on occasion, no regulation is sometimes proportionate. On occasion we should accept that we live in a world that will never be risk-free, and, therefore, we should not have risk-averse regulation because a risk-averse business world and, I would argue, on occasion a risk-averse public sector, ends in the public sector having a degree of mind-numbing uniformity and in the business world a stifled creativity, so proportion is what I would argue for. I think I have shared with your Lordship's Committee before my thoughts on being a better regulation minister or the proportionate regulation minister in Government a number of years ago, and I was asked about this in one of the sub-committees in your Lordships' House last week: I think the European Commission is making progress on better regulation but what progress does it have to make further? Its consultation has to be wider: it has to consult small businesses much more effectively: it has to ensure that impact assessments are the norm, I think there has been about 300 in recent years: and then they have to have post-implementation assessments of the accuracy of the impact assessments because it is well known to your Lordships that impact assessments are a prediction of what the best assessment is as to what should happen, but these things gain by being revisited after three or five years to see whether they were accurate predictions, because one can never make a judgment as to whether these predictions are

worth investing political capital in and whether they are accurate. I agree to monetarisation on the impact assessments: "This proposal will cost X euro or X pounds". That is what I would encapsulate as "better regulation".

Q22 *Lord Wade of Chorlton:* Do you think there is a further role that our European Committees could play in helping you to do a proper analysis?

Mr Murphy: Undoubtedly. Without question. A change has begun under the present Commission which has to continue under the new Commission when it takes up office next year. As I referred to earlier when I was asked for my priorities, the United Kingdom government, along with a number of other Member States, is genuinely passionate about this, not in and of itself because in and of itself it is often a relatively dry subject, but a better regulation agenda helps United Kingdom plc achieve so much else and can help Europe as well achieve so much more, which is why three weeks ago now I travelled to Prague and along with the governments of the Czech Republic and four other Member States we signed a declaration of continuing commitment on better regulation to continue to push the Commission and other Member States.

Q23 *Lord Wade of Chorlton:* I think you will agree that the use of the word "better" suggests it can be done differently than it has been done in the past, so clearly there is room for improvement and, clearly, that means room for a better understanding of what has taken place and how that can be amended?

Mr Murphy: All of that is true.

Q24 *Chairman:* Maybe what we need is for the better regulation portfolio to be handed over to a British commissioner. We seem to be the ones with our focus on this issue. The results have been pretty disappointing so far.

Mr Murphy: They have made, from a very low base— and I think it is important to reflect that it was from a very low base—progress, but not enough yet. With this Commission, from the President downwards, there is a determination to make progress but I think I have reflected with your Lordships before, and certainly I have with the sub-committees, that the Commission is a reflection on occasion of the demands of Member States and the "something must be done" tendency. We see a problem and "something must be done". Now on occasion nothing should be done.

Q25 *Lord Mance:* In the sub-committee, Sub-Committee E, you mentioned last week the subject of "less" Europe. Can I ask you about the main interest of that Sub-Committee, the area of freedom, security and justice? I think you indicated that this might be regarded as one of the priorities after climate change, but our sub-committee's comment was that it did not seem to be from reading the annual policy strategy, and I wanted to ask you some questions about the rather general and vague nature of what is said. At paragraph 2.4 we have "Work on the creation of a common area of justice will continue, in particular by ensuring the mutual recognition of judgments . . . and by improving access to justice . . ." Is there a problem in those areas, particularly in mutual recognition of judgments? There is a reference later in this strategy to modernising the Brussels regulation but I was not aware and I do not know whether the United Kingdom government has taken the view that there is a problem or who has suggested that. Access to justice is extremely broad. Then there is a reference in paragraph 2.7 to communicating better governance and policies in the area of freedom, security and justice, and I am a loss I am afraid as to what that might mean, and then there are the two specific references I mentioned in the annex, page 17, to Brussels regulation being modernised, which I think everyone would approve of but which is quite technical law, and simply a communication on the attachment of bank accounts, which is a pretty limited area. There is nothing on another area which has been in the news generally, that is the common frame of reference in relation to contract law, where nobody knows whether what is aimed at is some sort of draft Code or whether it is simply a toolbox for legislators in courts, and I am a little, therefore, puzzled as to where the input comes and whether there is any focus in the area.

Mr Murphy: Another one of those questions where I am invited to "discuss"! It is a remarkably broad area of work, of course. First, on fundamental rights, I know there were some observations about this issue and how the Explanatory Memorandum says no issues arise, but I want to put on the record that that is because the nature of the document is not a package of specific legislative proposals. Once the legislative proposals emerge this year and the first half of 2009, they will be relatively meagre as a consequence of so much else that is happening in Europe with a new Commission, a new Parliament, the Lisbon Treaty and everything else. In terms of this issue of justice and home affairs and common law and mutual recognition, I think it is a reflection of a degree of vigilance by Her Majesty's Government which is continually arguing the case for mutual recognition rather than harmonisation, and that is the purpose of this statement. It is not a statement where we detect additional pressure for harmonisation: it is a fair reflection of the fact that there is an absolute recognition of mutual recognition rather than harmonisation. On the issue of fundamental freedoms and justice and home affairs more generally, the Annual Policy Strategy is

relatively light, I think that is a fair reflection, largely because much of the work is contained in the five-year Hague programme of work, so most of the justice and home affairs issues are on-going as part of the four previous annual policy strategies, and I would be surprised, and I will happily come back and explain why I am surprised, if in the first few months of the advance of the Lisbon Treaty there is a substantial number of new justice and home affairs proposals, partly because the architecture governing justice and home affairs changes part of the Lisbon Treaty, and there will be a sense of let's allow the Lisbon Treaty architecture to bed down and then test the proposals in the context of that new architecture. So I think for these fundamental freedom issues and justice and home affairs it will be a relatively quiet period.

Q26 *Lord Blackwell:* I wonder whether in a way we are not all being too polite about this APS. The reality is that it is not seen as a document that plays any part in negotiating the Commission's remit or budget, the negotiation on what is in the programme is all done elsewhere, and therefore to that extent it is in effect a box-ticking government exercise where they try to put the minimum in it that will restrain their freedom of action. Against that observation I was also struck by the lack of any information about what their future plans were in criminal justice and civil justice; it may be, as you say, that they are waiting for the Lisbon Treaty to be ratified before they do that. Are you aware in that case that there is a backlog of proposals that they would want to bring forward once it is ratified? It does seem rather odd that they are saying how important it is to have these provisions in the Treaty if they do not have a long list of things they want to use them for once they pass the Treaty.

Mr Murphy: I think a lot of the energy and time over the next few years on justice and home affairs issues will be about taking existing policies from Pillar Three governance and transposing them into the Community Framework. If noble Lords wish to reflect on where is the substantial amount of future work planned perhaps over the next five years on justice and home affairs issues, a very good starting point I think would be the fact that 50[1] or so Pillar 3 policies areas currently have to be transposed over to a Community method; that is the substantial job that has to be completed over the next few years. Now, the important caveat I have to offer every time I say that is that, of course, the United Kingdom has its opt-out on each of those measures as they transpose over to the Community method, but alongside that there is a plan of work on the Hague programme, and I think your Lordships have previously had evidence about

---

[1] Subsequently corrected by witness—see supplementary memorandum

the work that is on-going in the Hague programme on counter-terrorism and on managed migration, so a lot of that work is on-going, but in terms of new energy I think it will be about transfer from Pillar 3 over to Community method on existing policies on justice and home affairs issues.

Q27 *Lord Blackwell:* If I could just follow on, if that is likely to be the priority area of activity here in the freedom and security and justice area over the next couple of years of the Lisbon Treaty the Government obviously will have to take a view on each one of those on what the position is and whether it is going to move the measure into the Community method. Is that an area that the Committees of this House and the other House with the Government should be thinking about and scrutinising in advance?
Mr Murphy: Absolutely, and Baroness Ashton is reflecting on this, with your own Committee and on the floor of the House of Lords. It is a new decision-making process that we are embarking on on the grounds of subsidiarity and other important matters, and I repeat this afternoon what I have said in the House of Commons, that it is important that we get it right from the beginning and that does mean an important role for the Select Committees of both Houses in the policing of these opt-in decisions, certainly.
Chairman: We had a lot of that yesterday, as you may know, in the Chamber.

Q28 *Lord Tomlinson:* I was very interested in the Minister when he was talking about better regulation, talking about revisiting some of the regulations every three and five years, that is a principle I am very, very strenuously in favour of, but I would like to see it applied in other areas as well. In budgetary terms, does the Minister perhaps sometimes favour getting the Commission to pledge itself to revisit budget lines on the basis of zero-based budgeting periodically, so that we can revisit them not necessarily every three to five years, a little less frequently, but taking a sample of budget lines which may well have outlived their utility if they are properly and objectively examined?
Mr Murphy: Without wishing to pre-empt the discussions that are going to take place on future budget perspectives, that is generally much of the approach the United Kingdom is going to take on this comprehensive review of the budget in advance of the next financial seven year perspective.

Q29 *Lord Tomlinson:* Well, I am prepared to leave it until you come back on that.
Mr Murphy: In seven years' time?
Lord Tomlinson: I am still planning to be around even if you are not, Minister, but warn your successor that the question will be there!

Q30 *Chairman:* Minister, one last question and then we will let you go. In two or three weeks' time I will be going to Edinburgh to talk to representatives of the devolved parliaments, and on the agenda is very likely to be the question of the degree to which they are kept informed of and consulted on the APS compared to the degree of consultation that takes place with the Westminster Parliament. It would be helpful to me if you could tell us to what extent your processes within the Foreign Office include talking to the devolved parliaments about the APS?
Mr Murphy: The main way of doing that would be through the Joint Ministerial Committee on Europe, that is the informal way as opposed to less formal structures, and the next meeting of the Joint Ministerial Committee is taking place within the next week or so. That is the structure and the most effective way of involving all devolved administrations. If, after your visit to Edinburgh, you have other reflections on the most effective way of doing it I, of course, am happy to have a conversation with you.

Q31 *Chairman:* But they will get the EM?
Mr Murphy: I would assume they will. They will get a package of information in advance of the joint ministerial committees, a copy of the documents, of the background documents and everything besides. There is a standing invitation, and perhaps we do not do this as regularly as we should, for the ministers in the devolving administrations to meet with myself in advance of the joint ministerial committees.

Q32 *Lord Roper:* But is there anything done at official level as well as at ministerial level in order to prepare responses to these documents?
Mr Murphy: I believe there is, yes. There is officials-to-officials dialogue but that is, as I say, a less formal way of doing it.

Q33 *Chairman:* At some stage we might like to learn a little bit more about the degree of consultation because it does come up all the time when we meet with our counterparts from the devolved parliaments.
Mr Murphy: It is right to come up, I think, and it will come up again on the issues of subsidiarity and how do we ensure there is a voice from the devolved administrations on subsidiarity issues.

Chairman: And it will also come on the question of scrutiny of opt-ins.

Lord Roper: Particularly because of the different systems for legal matters in at least one of the devolved administrations.

Chairman: So we are quite conscious of it. Minister, thank you for being generous with your time, as always, and thank you for answering our questions, as always, with lots of information and, if I may say so, good humour too. It is much appreciated.

Memorandum by Jim Murphy MP, Minister for Europe

2009 ANNUAL POLICY STRATEGY

I promised to write to you with further information on a number of issues of interest to the Select Committee, following my evidence session to your Committee on 10 June, on the European Commission's Annual Policy Strategy (APS) for 2009.

The Committee sought clarification on how the Government consults with the Devolved Administrations on our response to the APS and on European policy formulation more generally. I can confirm that the Explanatory Memorandum on the APS was shared with the Devolved Administrations in March. The JMC(E) Ministerial Committee is the primary means through which we discuss EU policy issues with the Devolved Administrations.

The Committee also asked about the extent to which Justice and Home Affairs policy would change under the Lisbon Treaty. I told the Committee that we expected around 50 proposals would need to be transposed over to the Community method from the Third Pillar. I have since been able to verify that the actual figure is 82. The resources needed to undertake this will limit the scope for additional initiatives in this field for some time to come.

I understand that the Committee had planned to ask a series of additional questions on various aspects of work planned by the Commission under the APS for 2009. I enclose details of the answers that I had planned to give the Committee during the evidence session, had time allowed.

3. *The Government's EM says that the APS has "no direct implications for subsidiarity". Individual proposals, of course, may well have subsidiarity implications. Which proposals do you intend to monitor closely to ensure that they add value at the European level?*

We pay particular attention, in our discussions with the Commission, to subsidiarity. The UK has long been a primary advocate of the principle of subsidiarity—going back to the 1992 Edinburgh European Council. The Protocol on Subsidiarity and Proportionality, introduced by the Amsterdam Treaty, was a UK initiative.

There are procedures in place to monitor subsidiarity. The Commission's Explanatory Memoranda include an assessment of compatibility with the principles of subsidiarity, proportionality and the conferral of powers. Usually the Commission gets it right, but there are occasions when its enthusiasm gets the better of it.

Subsidiarity can only be considered on the basis of an individual proposal for legislation. Concerns cannot be inferred from the APS alone, and it is difficult to predict, ahead of seeing an individual draft proposal, whether or not the UK would have concerns with regards to subsidiarity. Subsidiarity concerns tend to arise not in specific subject areas, but rather where there are horizontal provisions on harmonisation and the approximation of laws (eg, under Art 95 TEC). In the past, we have seen subsidiarity concerns in fields such as environment and employment legislation.

7. *Will 2009 produce any progress on reforming the EU budget?*

Discussions on long-term budget reform are being taken forward in the context of the European Commission's Budget Review.

HMG's response to the Commission White Paper set out a positive and principled vision for future EU budget Expenditure, in line with the agreed HMG EU Budget Review policy and consistent with our Global Europe agenda. It called for a fundamental re-orientation of spending away from agriculture and towards 21st century challenges: such as prosperity, climate change and poverty reduction.

Our principles for a modern budget are:

— first, the EU should only act where there are clear additional benefits from collective efforts or "EU added value", compared with action by individual Member States;

— second, where EU-level action is appropriate, it should be proportionate and flexible. We must recognise the limits to EU budgetary intervention. Expenditure is just one of a number of policy levers, alongside coordination, sharing best practice, and legislation or regulation. In addition, the full range of financing options should be considered, including both grant and loan finance; and

— third, sound financial management, including a modern approach to management and audit and greater focus on delivery of outcomes in programme design and evaluation. It will be important to maintain budget discipline.

11. *The Commission states that negotiations on a new round of Bilateral Free Trade Agreements will continue during the coming year, including negotiations on a new Partnership and Cooperation Agreement with China. How do these fit with efforts to conclude the Doha Round successfully? Do you share the Commission's belief that the Doha Round will be completed?*

The Doha Development Agenda remains the Government's trade policy priority. We are devoting a great deal of effort, from the Prime Minister downwards to ensuring that a deal can be reached in 2008. But for the deal to be concluded this year, significant progress, culminating in an outline deal on agriculture and industrial goods (NAMA), must be made in the next few weeks.

Pascal Lamy (Director General, WTO) believes a deal can still be done this year. The Government shares his confidence, but a lot of hard work and political commitment by leading nations is needed in the coming weeks.

With regards the Partnership and Cooperation Agreement, or PCA, with China, the UK has been active in shaping the vision for the development of EU-China relations, with the result that Community policy towards China is now more strategic and wide ranging, with the proposed PCA going well beyond the narrower scope of the 1985 Trade and Cooperation Agreement.

The Government believes that the PCA, covering co-operation, political and economic issues will guide the future scope, direction and parameters of the EU-China relationship and in particular supports strongly the trade and investment aspects of a future agreement, the key objectives being to:

— building on China's WTO commitments to remove restrictions on investment and foreign ownership in China, and

— obtain better protection of intellectual property and negotiate mutual recognition of geographical indications.

The EU also intends to address with greater intensity the:

— sustainability and environmental aspects and impacts of its economic and trade relations with China; and

— enhance cooperation on safety and health standards.

The Government does not see Free Trade Agreements as an alternative to the Doha Development Agenda, but believe that there is value in these agreements as long as they are complementary to what will be achieved in the Doha round.

12. *The APS includes a proposal that the fisheries and aquaculture Common Market Organisation be reformed. Are you aware of the Commission's motivation for the inclusion of this in the APS, and would the Government support, in principle, such a reform? Do you consider that it may be an opportunity to explore further the role of the EU in relation to the eco-labelling of fisheries products?*

The Commission conducts periodic reviews of the Common Market Organisation. The original aims of the CMO were to provide market stability and guarantee a fair income for fish producers. Supply is often not adapted to the needs of the market in terms of quantity, quality and regularity. This is partly due to the poor state of conservation of fish stocks. Improvements in international transport have encouraged an increase in imports of fish products. In addition, marketing structures have changed.

The result has been a growing dependence on imported fisheries products, which now account for more than 60% of total consumption in the European Union. There has also been an evolution from a market dominated by fresh fish to one where consumers have increasingly turned to processed fish products, especially prepared meals. Consumers have become more demanding, not only in terms of choice, but also in terms of the dietary and hygiene quality of food products.

A major reform of the CMO was undertaken in late 1999 with a view to achieving a better match between supply and demand, strengthening the competitiveness of the processing industry and improving information to consumers about the fish products available on the market.

Greater international competition means that the EU fishing industry must become more competitive by exploiting its strength, particularly in the fresh fish sector. This is more difficult to achieve in a situation of overcapacity, coupled with reduced fishing opportunities because of over fishing.

The Government firmly supports further reform, which is long overdue. We are fully supportive of the review to deliver the necessary improvements.

Reform will also be an opportunity for a greater focus on the consumption end of the fisheries marketing chain, linked to the promotion of fish as a healthy food source and eco-labelling will be a key element of this. The Commission are currently exploring the setting of appropriate standards for individual schemes within the Community, with this in mind.

The EU is already signed up to a basic framework for eco-labelling, established under the auspices of the Food and Agriculture Organisation (FAO) of the United Nations (UN). This is however extremely simple (in order to allow the participation of developing countries). Member States have therefore recently agreed that more stringent criteria should be established at Community level, whilst still providing an element of flexibility to allow them to develop their own bespoke national schemes.

The UK fully supports the principle of improving consumer information to assist purchasing decisions. However, we have resisted calls to be actively involved in the accreditation process for existing schemes like that of the Marine Stewardship Council—although we have provided some funding both to the MSC itself and to assist the provision of information to support applications for accreditation.

28 June 2008

WEDNESDAY 2 JULY 2008

Present	Cohen of Pimlico, B	Roper, L
	Freeman, L	Tomlinson, L
	Grenfell, L (Chairman)	Wright of Richmond, L
	Powell of Bayswater, L	

Memorandum by Commissioner Wallström, Commissioner for Institutional Relations and Communication Strategy, European Commission

REPLY TO QUESTIONS FROM THE HOUSE OF LORDS IN PREPARATION FOR THE EVIDENCE SESSION ON WEDNESDAY 2 JULY 2008

COM (2008)72 FINAL—ANNUAL POLICY STRATEGY FOR 2009

1. *Will the priorities listed in the Annual Policy Strategy make the European Union more relevant to European citizens? How will these priorities help the Commission address the credibility gap between the model of the EU and the public opinion of it?*

It is clearly the Commission's intention for 2009 to continue delivering tangible results on subjects that matter to the European citizens. The major proposals made by this Commission in the area of energy, climate change, migration and the management of borders, transport, telecoms, the internal market and consumer policy will have a direct, daily impact on Europeans. Recently, proposals for a renewed social agenda for the 21st century and the package of measures linked to the Small Business Act have added to the list.

The Commission's policy initiatives can play a significant role in illustrating the relevance of the EU to citizens, but they will always be only one part of the picture. It is essential that all the actors in the EU's system of governance—the institutions, the Member States, public authorities at all levels—work together to convey more effectively the realities of the EU's objectives, actions and results.

2. *Why are "Making a Reality of the Common Immigration Policy" and "Putting the Citizen First" key priorities for the Commission? What does "Putting the Citizen First" mean as a priority?*

Migration is currently one of the major challenges facing the EU as a whole. In December 2007, on the basis of the Commission Communication *Towards a Common Immigration Policy* (COM(2007)780), the European Council concluded that further developing this policy—which complements Member States' policies—remains a fundamental priority in order to meet the challenges and harness the opportunities which migration represents in a new era of globalisation. The European Commission fully shares this assessment and, accordingly, has made immigration a key priority in its Annual Policy Strategy for 2009.

The importance of immigration for the social, economic and political stability of the Union has been confirmed recently in the shape of the Commission Communication *A Common Immigration Policy for Europe: Principles, actions and tools* (COM (2008)359 and SEC(2008)2026), welcomed by the June European Council. A Common Immigration Policy is the best and in many cases the only way to address a number of very significant problems such as shrinking EU population and demographic ageing, labour and skills shortages, insufficient integration of legal immigrants, continuous pressure of illegal immigration, insufficient partnership with third countries or insufficient adaptation of border management and visa policy to the needs of a globalized world. This conclusion is echoed by EU citizens themselves: according to a Eurobarometer poll of November 2007,[1] EU citizens consider immigration the third most important aspect which should be emphasized by the European institutions in the coming years, to strengthen the European Union in the future (after the fight against crime and environmental issues).

---

[1]   http://ec.europa.eu/public_opinion/archives/eb/eb68/eb68_first_en.pdf

As regards the key priority *Putting the Citizen First*, it reflects the fact that one of the main objectives of this Commission is to put the citizen at the centre of the European project and to deliver policies which are relevant to their everyday lives. This priority involves policies in areas such as fundamental rights and citizenship, justice, security, consumer protection, and health and safety, which are of direct interest to citizens. There are naturally also overlaps with other priorities.

3. *The Commission's Annual Policy Strategy looked forward to a lull in 2009, with the European Parliament elections and the new Commission, and "a strong institutional framework in place". Will the contents of the Annual Policy Strategy have to be reconsidered in the light of the Irish referendum result?*

The Treaty of Lisbon would not in itself have affected the timing of the institutional changeover in 2009: the European elections and the arrival of the new Commission. So there will be no direct consequences from the Irish referendum result in this respect.

The Annual Policy Strategy is the first step of the Commission's programming cycle. It aims to launch a dialogue between the Commission and the other institutions, Member States and national parliaments on the main policy priorities to be taken forward next year. On the basis of this dialogue, the Commission draws up it Work Programme in the autumn. This process also gives a margin to react to developments right up to the adoption of the Commission Legislative and Work Programme.

Because the ratification process was still ongoing, the Annual Policy Strategy for 2009 took a prudent approach with regard to the Lisbon Treaty: it did not list in detail all the consequences of the entry into force of the Treaty or all the initiatives flowing from it. The nature and timing of such initiatives will clearly be subject to ongoing review.

4. *If there will still be a lull, how does the Commission want to use that time? Is it an opportunity for focussing on better regulation and implementation?*

The EU institutions do not cease to work in the year of an institutional changeover. However, the work of the European Parliament is interrupted for elections, and Commissions have traditionally sought to limit the launch of new proposals in the final months of their mandate. The Commission has sought to table most of its major outstanding legislative initiatives by 2008. In early 2009, the Commission will work closely with Council and Parliament to reach agreement on the most important pending proposals. It will focus on making sure the *acquis* is being properly implemented in line with the new approach agreed in September 2007.[2] And it will ensure that the financial programmes agreed for the period 2007–13 are managed effectively and efficiently and that financial programmes relating to the 2000–06 period are brought to a successful closure, in full accordance with the principles of sound financial management.

The Better Regulation Programme is one key way in which the Commission seeks to deliver results to citizens and businesses. In 2009, the Commission will continue to strengthen its impact assessment system and will continue to look for new simplification potential through the on-going screening of the existing body of legislation. At the start of this Commission's mandate, it screened pending proposals and withdrew a large number from consideration—the Commission intends to propose that its successor undertakes the same exercise. In addition, the Commission intends to present a substantial number of proposals in 2009 designed to reduce administrative burdens. At the same time, implementation of the Action Programme to reduce Administrative Burdens will be reviewed and progress in meeting the 25% reduction target for 2012 will be assessed.

5. *The Annual Policy Strategy calls for a "stronger presence of the Commission in international financial institutions". What does this mean? What in the Annual Policy Strategy indicates that the EU will be able to make an effective response to global financial instability?*

In this section, the Annual Policy Strategy refers to challenges to financial stability and global surveillance mechanisms. Finance Ministers of the G7 and Commissioner Almunia reaffirmed at their meeting in London on 9 February 2008 their support to the International Monetary Fund working closely with other international bodies (in *primis* the Financial Stability Forum) to set up an early warning system to better detect sources of vulnerability in the financial sector. They also expressed their support for the Commission becoming an observer of the Financial Stability Forum (FSF), which has been asked by the G7 to develop

---

[2]   COM(2007) 502, 5 September 2007.

responses to the lessons learned from the turmoil. Given the overlap between this FSF work and the work programme endorsed by the ECOFIN Council (see below), and the Commission's co-ordinating role, an observer status in the FSF seems necessary to ensure an adequate flow of information between the G7 and the EU.

Moreover, it should be recalled that the Commission has observer status in the Basle Committee on Banking Supervision. Both the Commission and the Basle Committee have benefited greatly from this arrangement. This is illustrated, for example, by the smooth implementation of the Basel II framework across the EU via the Capital Requirements Directive.[3]

Against this background, active participation of the Commission in the FSF meetings should be in the interests of all parties. The conclusions of the March 2008 ECOFIN Council have reiterated this position: "Considering the need to reach a global solution for many of the outstanding issues, close cooperation at international level is required especially with international standard setting bodies, in particular the Basle Committee on Banking Supervision, the International Organisation of Securities Commissions (IOSCO), the International Association of Insurance Supervisors (IAIS) and the International Accounting Standards Committee (IASC), as well as the Financial Stability Forum (FSF). The EU and EU Members States are engaged in discussions at international level in these different fora and, should actively promote European positions as reflected in this report. In this context, the Commission should participate in the FSF as soon as possible".

More generally, further to the ECOFIN Council discussions on 9 October 2007 in the wake of the financial turmoil, the Commission has been tasked with monitoring work in a series of areas (ie enhancing transparency, addressing valuation issues, strengthening prudential supervision of banks, and examining structural market issues) and with formulating and proposing appropriate policy responses. The Commission is currently working to ensure that the ECOFIN "roadmap" is delivered on time, including concrete initiatives on capital requirements and credit rating agencies.

6. *What real practical effect does listing an issue (eg immigration) as one of the Commission's priorities have?*

The practical effect of listing an issue as one of the Commission priorities in the Annual Policy Strategy is twofold: first, it allows the other institutions and the national parliaments to give their opinion on these priorities and make comments which will be taken into account when the Commission presents its Legislative and Work Programme in October. We attach great importance to this early dialogue on priorities for the upcoming year. The second effect is that the Commission commits itself to delivering on these priorities in making proposals or taking initiatives which directly respond to the priorities identified in the Annual Policy Strategy.

7. *Is there enough consistency between the priorities in the Annual Policy Strategy and the resources outlined in the preliminary draft budget?*

The Annual Policy Strategy constitutes the first stage of the annual budgetary cycle and determines the framework within which the Commission establishes the Preliminary Draft Budget. It sets out what specific initiatives the Commission will undertake every year in the broader context of the Commission five-year strategic objectives, and what resources are needed taking into account the multiannual Financial Framework. However, many initiatives considered in the Annual Policy Strategy have no budgetary impact.

In the Annual Policy Strategy for 2009, the Commission proposed the following three adjustments to spending programmes which have subsequently been confirmed in the 2009 Preliminary Draft Budget:

— The FRONTEX Agency's reinforcement of €30 million in 2009 in order to provide sufficient means to effectively contribute to the Common Immigration Policy;

— EU Strategy on Central Asia with €15 million in 2009, thus reinforcing the delivery of the objectives of the European Union in the region;

---

[3] Directive 2006/48/EC of the European Parliament and of the Council of 14 June 2006 relating to the taking up and pursuit of the business of credit institutions (OJ L 177, 30 June 2006, p 1–200) and Directive 2006/49/EC of the European Parliament and of the Council of 14 June 2006 on the capital adequacy of investment firms and credit institutions (OJ L 177, 30 June 2006, p 201–255).

— Environment and sustainable management of natural resources in line with the Bali Roadmap, with €10 million in 2009, thus contributing to the EU's objectives relating to climate change.

By confirming these adjustments in the Preliminary Draft Budget for 2009, the Commission ensures full consistency between the priorities of the Annual Policy Strategy and the resources allocated in this PDB.

As announced in its Annual Policy Strategy for 2009, the Commission requested in the 2009 Preliminary Draft Budget only the last 250 EU-2 related posts to cope with the enlarged Union. The Commission will serve all other priorities (the other 600 needs announced in the 2009 Annual Policy Strategy) by internal redeployment, notably to reinforce the priorities set out in its Annual Policy Strategy for 2009, including the Lisbon strategy for growth and jobs, enforcement of EU law, climate change, energy and migration.

8. *What responses to the Annual Policy Strategy does the Commission receive from Member State governments, and what does it do with them?*

The Commission receives a response from Member States assembled in the Council of Ministers (comments from the "Antici Group" composed of representatives of all Member States). The Commission systematically examines these contributions in the run-up to its Legislative and Work Programme which is presented in October each year and takes them into consideration when designing this Work Programme.

9. *What in the Annual Policy Strategy will lead to better energy security, and what in the Annual Policy Strategy indicates that the EU will be able to provide an effective response to high fuel and food prices—issues of great concern to European citizens?*

On the issue of pressure created by high prices for food and oil, the Commission has presented two communications on these subjects (COM (2008) 321 and 384) which served as the basis for the detailed discussions during the last European Council on 20 June. The discussions showed the importance of finding the right balance—of being able to demonstrate that Europe's political leadership was responding quickly to a genuine problem, whilst at the same time acknowledging the deeper challenge of adjusting to new realities for the long term. Commission action in the area of energy prices will include a package of measures to help fishermen face the need to restructure, and proposals on emergency and commercial oil stocks.

The European Council made clear that further efforts to improve energy efficiency and energy savings and efforts to diversify the EU energy supply remain essential in response to rising prices. It is therefore important to agree on the proposed EU policy for climate change and renewables, which would include policies that reduce oil and gas consumption in the longer term—and therefore increase energy security. It is also important to promote competition in the energy markets, and to enhance dialogue with oil exporting countries, in order to improve the framework conditions for investment in oil exploration and production, as well as in oil refining capacity. The European Commission and the incoming French presidency of the EU were also asked to examine the feasibility and impact of measures to smooth the effects of the sudden price increases, and will report back on this issue at their next meeting in October. The Commission will also monitor both food and oil price developments both in Europe and internationally and will report to the European Council in December this year. The European Commission is also working on the external aspects of energy security and intends to feed in ideas ahead of a discussion planned by the French Presidency at the European Council in December.

The Annual Policy Strategy for 2009 already includes many actions along these lines. Key actions for 2009 are the agreement on and implementation of the climate change and renewables package in the run-up to the UN climate change meeting in Copenhagen, the implementation of the Energy Efficiency Action Plan, the further boost of new energy technology development (including its financing), the extension of the Energy Observatory in charge of monitoring of main indicators of energy supply. Furthermore, the Second Strategic Energy Review to be tabled by the end of this year will address energy security issues. It will examine the need for better oil, gas and electricity interconnections within the EU and for diversification of sources and routes of supply; the need for gas storage and better oil stock mechanisms; the development of new technologies such as Carbon Capture and Storage and related infrastructure and finally the need to implement a common voice in our relations with third countries with the appropriate mechanisms. The Second Strategic Energy Review and supporting documents (Green Paper on trans-European energy networks, oil stocks directive, and security of gas supply report) should be discussed under the French and the Czech Presidency to help design a new Action plan for the period 2010–14 to be agreed at the European Council of March 2010.

10. *Can you explain the motivation behind the proposal that the fisheries and aquaculture Common Market Organisation should be reformed? Will the initiative provide an opportunity to make further progress on the eco-labelling of fisheries products?*

The current common market organisation (CMO) laid down in Council Regulation (EC) No 104/2000 is undergoing a comprehensive evaluation process which aims at assessing the effectiveness, efficiency, coherence, relevance and suitability of both the constituent parts of the CMO and the intrinsically related activities such as supply policy, consumer policy and international trade. Further to this, the evaluation of the financial instruments of the CMO is an obligation placed upon the European Commission under the terms of the Financial Regulation.

The evaluation consists of a series of studies which will be completed by the end of 2008. In addition, the Commission envisages a broad consultation of stakeholders so that they can provide input to the evaluation process. In the light of the results of the evaluation, the Commission may envisage proposals for a reform and revision of the CMO. It would be premature to speculate on what form these changes might take.

As regards eco-labelling, the Commission is moving forward independently of the above CMO review on the basis of the Council Conclusions of 16 April 2007. Following a period of reflection on the best approach the Commission plans to put forward a proposal for a new Public/Private Partnership in early 2009 to stimulate the creation of a sector-driven European standard for both wild fisheries products and aquaculture. This may or may not include EU legislation to establish the overall framework. European stakeholders (professionals, NGOs, independent and possibly national Eco-label schemes and consumer representatives) will be invited to participate. The entity would produce the minimum EU requirements for Eco-labels and provide the minimum principles for certification and accreditation which would remain Member State competence. The aim is to have a scheme based on a real partnership with industry and civil society which will be responsive and easily adaptable to the needs of industry (from fishermen to retailers) but take account of civil society aspirations.

11. *The Annual Policy Strategy contains little detail of the Commission's 2009 criminal and civil justice programme. What progress is expected in achieving the outstanding objectives of The Hague Programme in 2009 and what are likely to be the priorities? Why does the Annual Policy Strategy not provide more information on the Commission's plans in this area?*

The objective of the Annual Policy Strategy is to set out the broad policy outlines for next year. It does not set out in detail the precise nature and timing of individual initiatives for 2009. These will ultimately depend on a series of factors, including reactions and comments made by the other institutions, national parliaments and stakeholders, and the result of public consultations and impact assessments which the Commission undertakes on its major initiatives. The Annual Policy Strategy is a transparent way of flagging the Commission's intentions for a given year. Further details on individual initiatives will be presented at a later stage, when the Commission draws up its Work Programme for next year.

The Annual Policy Strategy for 2009 mentions several initiatives in the area of civil justice (Modernising the Brussels I Regulation on jurisdiction, recognition and enforcement of judgments in civil and commercial matters, Green paper on the legalisation of documents in the EU and Communication on the attachment of bank accounts). Besides these initiatives, the Commission will work on the following issues:

— A proposal for a Regulation on the conflict of law in matters concerning matrimonial property regimes, including the question of jurisdiction and mutual recognition, is being considered for adoption by the Commission by the end of 2009. This would be a follow-up to the Green Paper presented in 2006.

— In December 2008 the Commission will probably present a Report on the application of Council Directive 2004/80/EC of 29 April 2004 relating to compensation to crime victims. The report will assess the application of the Directive and evaluate it as an instrument to facilitate access to justice. This report, followed by a corresponding impact assessment and public consultation, may lead to a proposal to amend Directive 2004/80/EC, in particular to improve access to compensation in cross-border situations.

— The Commission will also follow up on the consultation launched by the Green Paper on transparency of assets presented in March 2008. Based on the results of this consultation, an impact assessment will be carried out in 2009 which may lead to a possible initiative at a later date.

As concerns criminal justice, the Commission is currently conducting a review of the implementation of mutual recognition in criminal matters, which may lead to a Communication in spring 2009. In parallel, the Commission is reviewing the implementation of some sectoral instruments, including the Framework

Decision on Freezing Orders, the Framework Decision on the standing of victims in criminal proceedings and the Framework Decision on the application of the principle of mutual recognition to financial penalties. The results of these reviews will be published by end 2008.

12. *The Annual Policy Strategy looks forward to a "Communication on sectoral social dialogue and its contribution to the Lisbon Strategy" in 2009. Why could this issue not be considered in the context of this year's Social Agenda?*

The proposed Communication on sectoral social dialogue has its origin in the Commission Communication of 20 May 1998 *Adapting and promoting the social dialogue at Community level* (COM (1998) 322) which created the current system of sectoral social dialogue committees through a Commission Decision (Annex II of the Communication). The system has expanded considerably, particularly in recent years. From the original nine committees, there are now 35 in operation and three in preparation, one of which will be launched on 1 July (Football). The Commission Decision provides for any review of the functioning of the Sectoral social dialogue to be carried out in close collaboration with the Social Partners. The Commission and the Social Partners consider that the experience gained to date with the sectoral social dialogue is sufficient to give a good basis for this review. A detailed examination of the functioning of the Sectoral social dialogue is therefore being launched now and the results of this consultation will only be available in the first half of 2009, which would allow the presentation of the communication in the second half of 2009.

It should be noted that there will already be a considerable social dialogue element in this year's Social Agenda package, with two significant documents. The Commission's report on the implementation of the Social Partners' Telework Agreement will present, for the first time, an analysis of the way in which an autonomous agreement of the European Social Partners has been implemented at national level. The Commission will also present a paper on the role of transnational company agreements, which are a major new element in promoting cross-border social dialogue.

13. *Why is there no reference to the European Security Strategy in the Annual Policy Strategy?*

While it is true that there is no explicit reference to the European Security Strategy in the Annual Policy Strategy for 2009, the text is referring in several instances to security issues and the Union's contribution to promoting international security and stability. It underlines the importance of energy security, climate change and migration as important guiding themes in external policy serving to strengthen the Union's commitment to effective multilateralism. The lack of a more specific reference is mainly due to the fact that, according to the conclusions of the European Council in December 2007, an improved and complemented European Security Strategy is scheduled for adoption already at the end of 2008. The Commission, which is fully associated in proposing elements to improve implementation and complement the Strategy, believes that this objective is both desirable and realistic, and is working effectively to support achieving it.

14. *The Annual Policy Strategy looks forward to savings of €20 million for large-scale IT systems (SIS II, VIS and EURODAC). How will these savings be realised?*

The financial programming concerning the large-scale IT systems (SIS II, VIS and EURODAC) was prepared in 2005 on the basis of best estimates and taking into account the level of prices in 2005. Certain actions initially foreseen in 2009 will not be carried out as they are not on the political agenda and/or no legal basis is available (passport database, various studies, and projects in the domain of border management). In addition, the development of the Biometric component of the VIS, the so-called BMS, is based on reviewed tariffs that have been decreasing taking account of the evolution of service prices in the IT sector.

The reduction, as presented in the Annual Policy Strategy for 2009, has absolutely no impact on the development/maintenance of the SIS II, VIS and EURODAC systems, which continue as planned.

15. *The Annual Policy Strategy states that spending on the Competitiveness for Growth and Employment and the Cohesion for Growth and Employment sub-headings will increase by 5.8% and 3.3% respectively. How will these funds be used?*

The increases foreseen in the 2009 Annual Policy Strategy for Sub-Heading 1a (Competitiveness for Growth and Employment) and Sub-Heading 1b (Cohesion for Growth and Employment) are in line with the medium-term financial programming of the different programmes and, therefore, fully coherent with the multiannual Financial Framework.

These increases have largely been confirmed by the Preliminary Draft Budget 2009:

— in Sub-Heading 1a the increase mainly results from a rise of Commitment Appropriations in the areas of research (+10.4% to €6.7 billion in 2009 for the Seventh Research Framework Programme), competitiveness and innovation (+17.2% to 483 million in 2009 for the Competitiveness and Innovation Programme—CIP) and education and training (+6% to 1.06 billion in 2009 for Lifelong Learning programme and Erasmus Mundus programme); and

— in Sub-Heading 1b the increase is mainly determined by a rise of commitment appropriations in the area of Regional policy (+ 14 % to 9.3 billion in 2009 for the Cohesion Fund and + 3.8% to 22.4 billion for the Convergence Objective of the European Regional Development Fund).

16. *What will "work on a renewed VAT Strategy" involve?*

The work on a new VAT strategy will be inspired in particular by the following aspects:

— the adoption of the VAT package by the Council in February 2008 has fully endorsed the approach to tax services in the place of final consumption; the major simplification proposal, the One Stop Shop has, however, not yet been accepted in its large conception; the further developing of this approach will therefore need to be one of the elements reflected;

— the debate on VAT fraud: it has shown that the VAT system is somewhat vulnerable and further work needs to be undertaken to define new approaches or working methods (like real time information of tax administrations) to provide for better protection; and

— the ongoing debate on reduced VAT rates and their use for other policy purposes (environment, energy saving, energy price smoothening etc) calls for a broad reflection on the possible evolution of this tax.

30 June 2008

Examination of Witness

Witness: COMMISSIONER WALLSTRÖM, Commission Vice-President for Institutional Relations and Communication Strategy, European Commission, examined.

Q34 *Chairman:* May I begin by thanking you for giving us this opportunity to talk to you directly. We are extremely grateful not only for the detail in which you answered our written questions, but also how quickly you got them to us.[1] I really wish our Government would be able to return answers to our questions with such speed. Thank you very much and many congratulations. As you know, we have read what you had to say. We would like this to be a free-flowing discussion as far as possible, so that we can get a broad view of what you feel about the Annual Policy Strategy, particularly in the light of what happened with the Irish referendum, but also go into one or two of the issues—not all of them, but the major issues—in a little more detail. I would like to know whether there is anything you would like to say to us to start with before we put a few questions to you.

Commissioner Wallström: Thank you very much, My Lord Chairman and honourable Members of the House of Lords. I appreciate it if we can set the standards when it comes to responding quickly for the UK Government, and I am glad that you appreciated the written replies we gave. This has now almost become a tradition for us, because it is the third time that we meet for evidence—although this time in a virtual way. I of course prefer the other

way—to meet in person—but I am glad that we have the opportunity. I also know that you have met twice with my head of Cabinet, Christian Leffler. If you will let me, I will just say a few words of introduction. I think the questions and replies provide good background for our discussion today. The objective of the whole Annual Policy Strategy is of course to spark a dialogue with the other institutions, with the Member States, and with the national parliaments on where the priorities should lie next year. This dialogue is also essential to ensure proper preparation of the Commission Work Programme for 2009. We are all aware that next year will be a special year, a transition year of great importance, marked by the end of the mandate of the Barroso Commission. The European elections in June will lead to a new European Parliament and we will also have a chance to celebrate 20 years of the march of freedom since the fall of the Berlin Wall. For next year the Commission will stick to its ambition of delivering a Europe of results and bringing concrete benefits to citizens. Let me remind you of the five pillars that make up the structure of the Annual Policy Strategy. The first priority is to promote sustainable growth and jobs; the second is to promote a low emissions and a resource-efficient economy; with the Common Immigration Policy being the third. The fourth pillar is to focus on delivering

---

[1] Printed at the end of this transcript.

policies of direct interest for citizens; for example, the revised social agenda. We discussed that and decided on that in the Commission meeting today—a whole package, a list of 15 different proposals, including one of patient mobility and, also, antidiscrimination legislation. Fifth, and finally, we will also pursue our objective of consolidating the role of Europe as a global partner. The international role we play will continue to be a very important one. In 2009 we will also be preparing the ground for the future financing of the Union's policies. The results of the consultation now underway on the budget review will help us to prepare the next multi-annual Financial Framework. That will be proposed by the next Commission, but I think this is important for you as well. Finally, the APS suggests a number of communication priorities for the year to come. This is hopefully the beginning of the programme, leading to the adoption of our Work Programme in October, so I think that this evidence session comes at a good moment. I really hope that I can answer any questions you might have. I can assure you that I will pass on your questions and concerns and comments to my colleagues in the Commission. Thank you for being there. I enjoy meeting you, even though it is the virtual way.

Q35 *Chairman:* Thank you very much indeed. The first question I want to put to you is in a sense a rather generic one. We are still wrestling a little bit with the ultimate objective of the APS. We had a discussion about this a year ago, but there is one thing on which we would like some clarification. Is this a political clarion call on the priorities of Europe in the coming year which is directed to the citizens of Europe, or is it more of an internal working "to do" list? The reason I ask this is because, obviously, with the result of the Irish referendum, the need to be able to explain the European Union to European citizens is extremely important. Are you appealing with the APS over the heads of the institutions to the European citizens, saying, "This is what needs to be done and it is up to the Member States and the institutions to make sure that it is done?" You have the right of initiative in the Commission and you are saying, "This is what needs to be done". If it is not done, then at least you can say, "Well, we proposed it, but it was not carried through, so don't blame us." To what extent are you appealing over the heads of the Member States to the citizens of Europe? To what extent are you in fact setting a work programme which will be spelled out in the annual Legislative and Work Programme for the institutions themselves?

Commissioner Wallström: That is, My Lord Chairman, as usual, a very clever question and at the same time a very political one. What we do with the APS is, of course, to flag up our intentions and, also, to start a dialogue with the other institutions, but I do not think you can ever disconnect it from what we want to signal to the citizens. It always has to be integrated into our Work Programme. In a way, it is both: it is to say that these are the political priorities of the Commission and this is how we want to engage also with institutions to carry out a programme which will be in the end good for our citizens. I think the best end result is the one that can integrate the two aspects. But it is really to start the co-operation with the other institutions because we need them to be able to do something or to deliver results with the citizens.

Q36 *Chairman:* We are in day two of the French Presidency. There is an ambitious programme there, set by President Sarkozy and his Government. Not everything will be completed in six months, though obviously the big issues which he is tackling, like immigration, climate change, security, et cetera, will spill over into 2009. To what extent can the Commission, in setting its Annual Policy Strategy, take into account the priorities of a particular presidency? How much communication is there? Because obviously what they are going to propose and what they would like to get done will spill over into the 2009 programme.

Commissioner Wallström: Of course, we are here to ensure there is a continuity. The different Presidencies have a trialogue, they have a way to co-operate so that they can also ensure the long-term planning, so that things are not interrupted every six months but instead follow an agenda that stretches over three presidencies. The same thing has been done now. We work very closely with these trialogues, or this triangular planning of the Work Programme, to try to ensure there is no interruption. Of course every presidency tries to bring their profile or their weight to some particular issues, but we cannot have that kind of interruption or total change of direction every six months. For example, the whole climate change and energy package with the French will continue and, hopefully, bring that to a successful decision and action from the Member States' side and from the Council's side. I can report from yesterday—because every time the whole Commission travels to the Presidency, and we went to Paris yesterday and we met with the whole French Government. It was a very ceremonial and solemn day, I would say, under a sunny sky in Paris. They made the most out of it, I must say, but it was clear that there is a list of very difficult issues. My experience is that we are never able to plan for the unexpected and there is always something unexpected that comes up during every presidency. That is what I can say about the plan.

Chairman: Thank you.

Q37 Lord Powell of Bayswater: Commissioner, I would like to follow up of your last answer. Clearly quite a few of the French Presidency's priorities are closely aligned with the Commission's document. On the other hand, as you say, there are always surprises. One of the surprises was the rather incendiary, provocative remarks of the President of France on the Doha Round. Do you see this as liable to throw out one of the commission's main priorities, which is to bring a successful conclusion to the Doha Development Round?

Commissioner Wallström: No. Of course we are discussing this, and I am sure that this was also one of the subjects for the discussions between our President and the French President last night at the dinner. But of course we do not accept that things are thrown out suddenly. These are very often processes that have been going on for several years, where we invest a lot and where other Member States also have a say. I think our role is very often to try to provide a good direction, to try to help, to mediate sometimes between Member States and sometimes, also, to calm things down—maybe to put some oil on . . . What do you say . . .?

Q38 Lord Powell of Bayswater: Oil on troubled waters.

Commissioner Wallström: Yes, exactly.

Q39 Chairman: Perhaps we should not mention oil here!

Commissioner Wallström: No, with the price of oil we cannot use that at the moment. We have a clear mandate. In many of these international negotiations we have a mandate which has been formulated and accepted by the Council as well. It is not something you can suddenly abandon and go for something else. This is what we have, to steer the way we act in the Commission as well.

Chairman: Thank you very much indeed.

Q40 Lord Wright of Richmond: Commissioner, you gave us a very helpful written answer to our question three about the Annual Policy Strategy and the implications of the Irish referendum result. I would like to ask two supplementary questions to that. In your introduction today you told us that you hoped that this would spark a dialogue and you have talked about launching a dialogue in a written reply. Where has the dialogue got to? Are we still at the beginning, or have you, other than this witness session, started a practical dialogue?

Commissioner Wallström: I think we are at the start of this dialogue. We are receiving from different national parliaments, for example, their comments, and their positions on this, so we are engaged in a constant dialogue also with the national parliaments. So far, we have had four replies from national

parliaments. That is the latest figure. Of course, with the European Parliament we have wanted to make this a process which is political; more than entering into details where the different committees will ask, "Why don't you have this proposal on insurance companies" or whatever, but rather, "Are these the right priorities?" and "Do we see that we can change this whole European project further?" This is still something we are struggling with, to make it a more political process also in the European Parliament. But with national parliaments it has started.

Q41 Lord Wright of Richmond: One of our questions was: "Will the contents of the Annual Policy Strategy have to be reconsidered in the light of the Irish referendum result?" to which you said, "The Treaty of Lisbon would not in itself have affected the timing . . ." Can you add anything to our question about contents?

Commissioner Wallström: It would have been on the implementation. We were preparing for, though not anticipating, implementation measures. I can give you one example. We had already planned in the autumn to discuss with the Parliament and to call for a stakeholder conference on the citizens' initiative. To have the citizens' initiatives implemented we would have needed to prepare a proper proposal from our side, including all the rules for how to control the number of signatures and what would be the role of the institutions, the Commission, and the Member States, et cetera. That would have had to be prepared in the autumn to be presented early next year. This, of course, we cannot do as the situation is now. So there could be separate implementation measures, in particular, that would have to be taken up.

Q42 Lord Wright of Richmond: Thank you very much.

Commissioner Wallström: Of course it will affect a whole debate about appointments, the new posts and all of these things, so there are also some rather dramatic effects. That is an overall concern for the whole of the European Union and not so much on the very practical proposals, I could say, but it affects the whole political debate and atmosphere.

Lord Wright of Richmond: Thank you.

Q43 Lord Powell of Bayswater: I have one supplementary question on that point, Commissioner. Suppose, for a moment, the Commission and the European Union's efforts to reach a solution which allows Ireland to ratify the Treaty do not succeed, is the Commission doing some contingency planning as to how certain portions of the Treaty could be brought into effect without needing to have a treaty which is ratified?

Commissioner Wallström: There is no alternative plan worked out. I think everybody has been so engaged now in trying, first, to negotiate this new treaty and then to have it ratified and, also, to start to look, in case of ratification from all Member States, at what we have to do in terms of implementation. That is where we have focused our attention and our efforts. If this fades, then we have to rethink the whole situation of course. But there are a few things. If it is not entering into force next year, there is, for example, one provision in the current treaties which talks about the number of Commissioners, for example, and this is something that will have to be solved. There are a number of questions that have to be discussed, but I think everybody prefers not to engage in some kind of alternative plan but focus on ratification and solving the problems that we see right now.

Q44 *Chairman:* Could I come back one of the two priorities which you listed in the APS, Putting the Citizen First. I have been looking at the report which Alain Lamassoure has presented—which of course is made to the French Government but does have some major implications for Europe as a whole. It identifies a certain number of problems experienced by Europeans in understanding the European Union and I wonder whether you are taking this on board and whether you are reacting to it, albeit that it is a report to the French Government from a French Member of the European Parliament.
Commissioner Wallström: Of course I have met with him: he came to see me. Indeed, the things that he will bring up are very interesting and accurate as well. I think we use every opportunity to be inspired or to learn the lessons from those who work on issues like this. I hope that we can make full use of the work that he has been doing for the French Presidency and we are in touch with him, without being able to say something very, very concrete. Of course the Better Regulation Agenda is already one of the points that we are working on. We have already integrated better regulation into our daily work in the DGs as part of our political priorities, so that is definitely one thing.
Chairman: Thank you very much.

Q45 *Lord Tomlinson:* Commissioner, I would like to follow up on this idea of Putting the Citizen First, linking it to the discussion we were having in relation to the outcome of the Irish referendum. In the analysis that the Commission are making and linking those two ideas together, what is the general attitude of the Commission? Is it that Ireland have not understood you? Or is it that you have not understood Ireland?
Commissioner Wallström: Some people put it even more bluntly. They say, "Why don't you take no for an answer? What is it in "no" that you don't

understand?" Then we say, "Well, no is an answer, but it is not a solution." We did immediately one of these sort of flash Euro-barometer polls, an opinion poll that could make us understand why did people vote yes and why did they vote no in Ireland, to better understand the different reasons and the motivations. We found a whole range of reasons why they said no. It was also an important element that this was in no way a no to the European co-operation or the EU membership in Ireland, because even the "No" side argued, "The EU has been good for Ireland; let's keep it that way." It was clear that this is not a general EU-sceptic mood in Ireland but, rather, I would say, many different motivations. It was clear, also, that the political context had been maybe more important than the text as such. As always, when you asked, a rather higher proportion of the "No" voters would say, "We feel that we don't know enough, that we can never get enough information." It is a complex legal text and, whatever you do, of course not everybody will have read it, so you will always ask for more information. But then came a number of reasons: everything from the risk of losing Irish identity, to the trade issue or agriculture, or a number of different reasons why they voted no. They all agreed that the "No" campaign had better arguments and a better campaign than the "Yes" side, and, of course, also that they were not pleased with the national politicians and it was a kind of protest vote against the politicians. We have to understand why they said no. Is this something we can help, because it affects the rest of Europe. It will affect those 19 Member States that have ratified, and the ones that have not yet ratified will also want to have their say. This is exactly what is going on right now. The Irish themselves have to make the analysis and come back and tell us what they think is the way forward. Was this an end of it? Or is there a way to solve some of the problems being raised and some of the reasons behind the "No" votes? I think this is a natural way of handling a situation like this: better understand the reasons and see if there is a way to remedy or to overcome the problems.

Q46 *Chairman:* Thank you very much, Commissioner. I am not sure whether I agree with the statement that the "No" vote had the better argument, but that is what you said. I would say that they had the louder arguments, but based on some rather strange theories.
Commissioner Wallström: But, you know, it is always more effective of course to mobilise fear for change. I think this is a natural streak in all of us, that we fear change. If this has been good for Ireland, then the argument "Let's keep it that way" was an effective one. Also, on the fear for changes that the new Treaty would bring, it was more emotional than the "Yes" side and the arguments that the "Yes" side used, so I

think it hit home in a more effective way. What was very worrying was of course that the young people were very negative and also women. Those were among those who did not vote. This is something we recognized from both France and the Netherlands, that women and young people feel apparently detached from very much of the political process or the European project. This is something that we have to take seriously. What are we doing wrong?

Q47 Lord Roper: Commissioner, in your second answer you discussed the question of immigration. The French Presidency has suggested that an immigration pact is one of the things which they intend to put forward. Has the Commission had an opportunity to discuss with the Presidency the interaction between your proposals and the ideas which the Presidency has in this matter?
Commissioner Wallström: I am convinced that, yesterday, in the bilateral meetings or cluster discussions that the Commissioners had with their counterparts in the French Government, this was raised. I was not in that particular cluster, but this of course will be part of the agenda where we now have to co-ordinate with the French Presidency. This is important, also, from a timing point of view: when can certain proposals be presented, how will they work on it, and what can we anticipate? This particular issue of the pact will also be discussed at the informal Council in Cannes—which is next week—so already next week the pact idea will be discussed at an informal Council.

Q48 Baroness Cohen of Pimlico: We asked about the stronger presence of the Commission at international financial institutions. It seemed to me that your written answer really says that the answer to the question is that the Commission should have an observer's place on the Financial Stability Forum. Is it now agreed by the other members of the forum that the Commission should have an observer's place or is it merely a hope on the part of the Commission? It seems like a very good idea.
Commissioner Wallström: This is how we see it. That is the Commission's position but, also, we are looking for support from the Member States for that. Not yet, but this is what we have put on the agenda. This is our starting point. We have discussed and presented these issues, I think at two occasions recently, and this is part of the package that we have prepared, that Almunia, McCreevy and others have discussed and prepared. Not yet, but this is what we are looking for Member State support for.

Q49 Baroness Cohen of Pimlico: I see that ECOFIN suggested that the Commission should participate in the Financial Stability Forum as soon as possible. Are observers allowed to participate? Does that

work? Or does the Commission really want a place in the forum? May an observer speak in this forum or must it merely sit and observe?
Commissioner Wallström: They can speak.

Q50 Baroness Cohen of Pimlico: Thank you. But the Commission does not yet have clearance for this and requires support.
Commissioner Wallström: Exactly.

Q51 Lord Freeman: Commissioner, good afternoon. Thank you for a very helpful answer to point nine on energy. Clearly 2009 is going to be a year of concern, not only to European citizens, about energy security and about climate change, but also to the French Presidency in the six months prior to 2009. How important, in terms of policy initiatives, will be a follow-up to what we assume will be agreement at the December Council on energy efficiency targets, energy renewable targets, and, indeed, other related issues all to do with fuel prices?
Commissioner Wallström: I think we cannot overestimate the value of this discussion and the decisions that we are taking. I can only follow the media in the different Member States. These are the headlines. These matters are at the top of the political agenda in all the Member States right now. It feeds into and leads to debates on oil prices, on food security. All of these issues are interlinked and this is why it is extremely important. We of course hope that we will have a successful result from the December meeting. We would also underline implementation, because we want all Member States not only to decide and establish great objectives and goals but also to start implementation as soon as possible. That is what I can say. I really see that it leads into all these other debates as well and maybe allows us to have a more holistic political debate on these issues.

Q52 Chairman: On the question of enlargement, you made it perfectly clear in the Annual Policy Strategy that you wanted to implement the renewed consensus on enlargement and that accession negotiations with Croatia and Turkey would continue. President Sarkozy and, it appears, also, Chancellor Merkel have said that there can be no further enlargement without the necessary reforms being put into place. I know that President Barroso and your colleague Olli Rehn and some governments like our own Government here are on the record as saying, "Sorry, Sarkozy and Merkel, but they are going to go ahead." I just want your view on this. Is it the Commission's view that there should be no interruption in the accession negotiations, and that if, for example, Croatia were to complete the negotiations in 2009, while the institutional reforms may not yet have been put in place and if the Lisbon Treaty has not been implemented, nonetheless, this would not be a block on them coming in, in 2010?

Commissioner Wallström: As all of you are very aware, this is a decision that has to be taken unanimously by Member States to change anything or to decide on enlargement. We have made very clear and strong commitments towards Croatia and Turkey. That is why we have started these negotiations and membership negotiations, and they follow very clear criteria and clear rules. We have no intention of changing that commitment, but to engage the way we have started. If Member States want to change that, it takes a unanimous decision by the Council. But, of course, the current treaty provides the legal framework and this also has to be obeyed and followed. This is where the rules are set on how to continue. My impression is that we continue, and we follow the commitments we have made and we follow the structure of these negotiations that have been started.

Q53 Lord Wright of Richmond: Commissioner, I would like to follow up the question from Lady Cohen about financial institutions. You have explained very clearly in your reply your role with the Financial Stability Forum, with the Basle Committee on Banking Supervision, and so on. Does this in fact reveal a desire to become more closely involved with the main institutions, with the IBRD, with the IMF? Do you have it in mind, possibly, even to have representatives attending their meetings?

Commissioner Wallström: I am glad that you think that I have the capacity to answer all of these very detailed and good questions on any subject—which of course I do not have the competence of doing. What restricts us as the Commission is, of course, where the European Commission has competence; otherwise, it has to be left to the Member States. I think the general discussion has been very much about some of the guiding principles of more *haute finesse* and better control, and, also, to make sure we play our role properly—like being an observer and so on. But we cannot expand on our competence without having changed things in the treaty or the legal framework. That is how the debate has been going.

Q54 Lord Powell of Bayswater: Commissioner, I would like to go back for one moment to your written answer to question eight, where you said that the Commission systematically examines contributions from the Member States on the Strategy and takes them into consideration when drawing up the Legislative and Work Programme. Would you or your colleagues be able to point me to one or two examples where the Commission has significantly changed the proposals and policies set out in the APS in response to Member States' suggestions?

Commissioner Wallström: I guess that what we discussed and debated and decided today in the Commission is one example; that is the social issues and the social package. That was introduced last year and, also, in part of some of the seminars that we had in the Commission as well. This was not initially in our proposal, but clearly became one of the demands from Member States to achieve a better balance. It is not only on the internal market and the growth in jobs, but it is also about social protection. This reflects, also, a changed political agenda, if you like, in political discussion and atmosphere. In the light of globalisation, this became much more pressing, to make sure that we clarified the laws and rules on antidiscrimination, for example, or the protection of workers. Maybe that is the clearest example.

Q55 Lord Powell of Bayswater: Could I go back to one of your other earlier answers, when we were dealing with Ireland and you said the Commission was very sensibly examining the many reasons why the Irish voted, by a majority, "no". Presumably it must worry you, as Commissioners, that on the occasions when people are consulted in referenda they generally do say no, whether it is the French or the Dutch or others. Do you think, from your examination, that the reasons are mostly about the general direction in which the European Union is moving or do you think it is more down to an inadequacy of communication to people of the reasons for the Community's policies? Or do you think that most of the reasons are nothing much to do with Europe but just with people taking revenge on their governments or other sorts of extraneous reasons? Where do you think the balance lies?

Commissioner Wallström: That is a €1 million question, almost, today. It is a very relevant question. I counted, and it turns out that Member States have arranged 15 referenda on treaties: 10 have given a yes, and in five cases there has been a no; so it is not entirely true to say that every time you arrange a referendum people voted no. This is not exactly correct.

Q56 Lord Powell of Bayswater: I think I said recent referenda.

Commissioner Wallström: Yes. Of course this is exactly the kind of analysis we are doing right now. I think it also has to do with the nature of putting a question like an international treaty of several hundreds of pages, to a referendum. In many Member States they would choose something a bit more manageable or a question that can be more easily interpreted to a referendum, where you can provide the information. The upside of a referendum is that you are obliged to inform citizens, to provide them with proper debate and all the information they need, but on an issue like this it will always pose an enormous challenge to make sure that people have read the text. You always risk having it sort of contaminated by all other things. We know fairly well through opinion polls what were the reasons behind the noes. There were different reasons, for example, in the Netherlands and in France and in Ireland. In France, you could see that there were very specific reasons, like the social issues, behind the noes, and in Holland there were other more specific issues. In Ireland, right now, it is much more diverse. It goes in all directions, right now, and it has also been affected by the general political climate and atmosphere in Ireland. I think it is a mix of the things you have mentioned yourself, and the inherent problems with such a complex issue to interpret the results is. I think it is a mix of all these things.

Q57 Lord Powell of Bayswater: It is of course difficult to get even ministers to read the Treaty let alone the general public.
Commissioner Wallström: This is one of the arguments used.
Chairman: That is why we did an impact analysis of the Treaty here in the House of Lords, in our Committee. The hope was that this would be useful to the House of Lords when they debated the ratification of the Treaty, in having what we would like to think was a very, very, objective explanation of what the Treaty was all about. But that came to nearly 300 hundred pages, a simple explanation of what it was without any value judgements. There is a problem there about what you present to the public.

Q58 Lord Tomlinson: Perhaps I might add, My Lord Chairman, that it produced some very good voting results in the House of Lords. We might consider selling the package to the Commission, so that they can use it to help them through their dilemmas in the countries that might have to rethink their views!
Commissioner Wallström: It would be highly appreciated! Thank you!

Q59 Lord Tomlinson: I am going to turn back to written question seven. Your written answer to question seven was about consistency between priorities in the Annual Policy Strategy and the resources outlined in the Preliminary Draft Budget, and you give us three examples of it. But perhaps I could preface my remarks by making a criticism about the whole Annual Policy Strategy process. I appreciate what is intended, but there seems to be almost an inevitable consequence that we get something at such a level of generality that it is very, very difficult to identify a policy strategy. We can identify a subject word, but very rarely a policy strategy to go with that subject word. I will give you one example and ask you to comment on it. If we are really going to do those two things, have a Common

Immigration Policy and Putting the Citizen First, I suggest that possibly public opinion in the United Kingdom would express its concern about the pattern of immigration into the United Kingdom following enlargement. The pattern of migration has changed radically. That would have consequences, if we followed it to its logical conclusion of putting the citizen first, of maybe questioning a policy that I do not want to question, which is the enlargement of the European Union in the Balkans. Because there is no doubt that if we canvassed public opinion in the United Kingdom, mass migration from the Balkans would be seen as a major immigration policy. We have all these words dotted about, but we do not have them as coherent policies that we are advocating. I want to know how we can get an Annual Policy Strategy that does not put in a little mention for every Commissioner's area of interest but really does focus on two or three priorities and takes the title beyond a title into an explicit view of what it is that you want to do?
Commissioner Wallström: I think the easiest thing for me is to agree very much with you.

Q60 Lord Tomlinson: Okay—you have won me over!
Commissioner Wallström: This, again, is an inherent problem of the timing of any policy strategy of this nature, because it also has to be combined and seen in the context of a five-year plan for a Commission, like the Barroso Commission, which tries to set out a long-term agenda for the five years' mandate. We try every year to translate that into a bit more detailed planning and then we go into the Legislative and Work Programme with even more details. It is always a delicate balance to strike here, to see that we have the right level of detail and, also, to allow for a proper political discussion on the priorities. Yes, there are inbuilt conflicts like the one you mention, but of course we deal with everything, as I usually say, from counting cod fished in the Baltic Sea to fighting famine in Africa. If we do all these things, there will always be enough to say this is a citizens' agenda because we deal with food safety, with toy safety, with passenger rights, things which are very, very close to citizens' hearts, which they can see in their everyday lives are important. At the same time you have the bigger picture of immigration. Of course, for politicians and political leaders it is a matter of not only following public opinion but also leading, and explaining, for example, the benefits of enlargement and how this has helped both development in the countries where they have come from and the countries in which they very often work. I think this is something we have to improve. We have not been able to explain well enough the benefits of enlargement. The benefits are overwhelming. All the statistical facts show that this has been beneficial to

Europe. We have ended the division of Europe into an East and a West. That is a fantastic achievement for our generation and for our generation of politicians.

Q61 *Lord Tomlinson:* My problem, Commissioner, is that I have looked back at this exercise last year and the year before, and I say, "Apart from the Lisbon Treaty, what was priority last year?" It has not made a great impact on me. And if it has not made much of an impact on me, I would suggest it has probably passed the average citizen totally by. What was our big idea for 2007? I have forgotten it. You probably have not; but if I have forgotten it, I would suggest that most of our citizens have.

Commissioner Wallström: We return to My Lord Chairman's first question in a way. We have gone the whole circle around. This means, also, the planning possibility for the institutions, of course, to set them on an agenda, and at the same time we want to communicate to citizens. What citizens will remember is what we do on energy and climate change—that we have addressed that, that we are doing something on biofuels—or where we are visible with things that are very, very concrete. This is what citizens will see, and very few, as you rightly say, will remember that as part of a five-point agenda or whatever. We win democratic legitimacy by doing the right things that really change the lives of European citizens. That is how we win legitimacy.

Q62 *Chairman:* Before asking Lord Roper to ask what may be the last question, could I say Commissioner that if any member of the public were to ask me, "What is in the Annual Policy Strategy? How can we understand what it is all about?" I would hand them the nine pages that we have here of our questions and your answers, which is half the length of the Annual Policy Strategy itself. I think it sets out admirably what the intentions of the Commission are. That is a way of saying that it is hard to sell an Annual Policy Strategy. It is not that it is 18 pages long but that, for the citizens, it should be in the form of questions and answers. What is it you are planning to do about this and that? Then you get the answers. This excellent document, which you sent us, of questions and your answers, is the best guide I have seen to the APS since you started having one. I say that in terms of congratulations and thanks to you, because it has made our job of getting our heads around this strategy a lot easier.

Commissioner Wallström: Thank you very much. Could I say, also, that I am very proud that we have started with something else; that is citizens' summaries. For all proposals that we prepare to send to the Parliament and to the Council we have to attach a citizens' summary which is a one-page description of the proposal. Why is it needed? Who will be affected? What does it mean? When will it enter into force?

Q63 *Lord Roper:* Commissioner, quite rightly in your thirteenth answer you say that there is no detailed reference for the European Security Strategy because that is going to be reviewed by the end of this year. To some extent, the European Security Strategy acts as an instrument to ensure that there is coherence between the various Community institutions when it comes to external actions, and you refer to some of them in your answer. I notice that there is one which you do not refer to, that is sometimes referred to as the security-development nexus, or, in another way— the sort of documents which were prepared under the Portuguese Presidency and which are being followed up—the policy towards fragile states, which obviously involves development and economic matters as well as security matters, and therefore combines operations coming from the Council as well the Commission. Do you not feel that this is another matter which ought to be mentioned and included in the discussion of the strategy for next year?

Commissioner Wallström: As they say: "Thank you very much for this question." I think you are more of an expert in this particular field, but I think we have to note this. I remember a discussion in the Commission also covering the issue of fragile states, but I am afraid that I do not know enough of the details of the strategy to be able to comment. We will take it with us. We will follow up and ask exactly where this issue is right now. Do you want us to come back with a reply?

Q64 *Lord Roper:* I was in Brussels and talking to Mr Popovska in the Development Director-General this week and they are doing some further case studies on it in a number of countries, but it is something which I think is very much on the agenda for next year and I therefore feel it is a pity that it was not included in this document.

Commissioner Wallström: I take your point and we will report back on this.

Q65 *Lord Freeman:* I know that governments respond to the Annual Policy Strategy. Are there any other consultations from parliaments or the private sector?

Commissioner Wallström: I mentioned at the beginning that we have received four opinions from national parliaments as well. More and more we are invited to present the strategy to national parliaments, so I think this will increase. I hope so, because this exactly the idea, that we will spark this dialogue and get input from both national parliaments as well as Member States' governments.

Q66 *Chairman:* Commissioner, Madam Vice-President, I thank you very, very much indeed for spending this hour with us. Even in the virtual fashion that we have done it, it has been extremely helpful to us. I hope that our questions to you have indicated what our concerns are. I think you have met many of them. We wish you well, particularly during this rather difficult period following the Irish referendum. We look forward to further contact with you, because direct contact with the Commission has enormously helped us in our work. We are extremely grateful for the Barroso initiative and all the other ways we have been able to communicate with you. The availability of your Commissioners to give evidence to our Sub-Committees and to our Select Committee is highly appreciated, and we can assure you that we will remain what they call in France *interlocuteurs valables*. We thank you very much indeed.

Commissioner Wallström: Thank you very much My Lord Chairman and honourable Members. I never thought I would say this, but I have appreciated all the contacts and the hearings also from you. Thank you very much. It is on behalf on my collaborators here as well. I feel that we have not only interlocutors but also allies and friends over there.

Q67 *Chairman:* You do.

Commissioner Wallström: Thank you very much. I hope we meet in person next time.

Printed in the United Kingdom by The Stationery Office Limited
7/2008 404017 19585

ISBN 978-0-10-401336-6

9 780104 013366